Time Flies When You're Having Fun,
and When You're Not

Time Flies

When You're Having Fun, and When You're Not

AL CADENHEAD, JR.

BROADMAN PRESS
NASHVILLE, TENNESSEE

© Copyright 1991 ● Broadman Press
All Rights Reserved
4260-17
ISBN: 0-8054-6017-9
Dewey Decimal Classification: 646.7
Subject Headings: TIME MANAGEMENT
Library of Congress Catalog Number: 90-39524
Printed in the United States of America

Library of Congress Cataloging-in-Publication Data

Cadenhead, Al, 1947-
 Time flies when you're having fun, and when you're not / Al
Cadenhead, Jr.
 p. cm.
 ISBN 0-8054-6017-9
 1. Christian life--Baptist authors. 2. Time--Religious aspects-
-Christianity. I. Title.
 BV4501.2.C22 1991
 248.8'4--dc20   90-39524
                                                        CIP

*To Chris and Melody who have filled my
time with joy*

C O N T E N T S

FOREWORD

When I say that this is not a simple book nor is the read
ing of it a simple experience, I mean it as a genuine
compliment to the manuscript and its author. Al Caden
head has undertaken a demanding challenge in these pages.
Of all the issues that humans face intellectually, I know of
no subject more puzzling or complex than the reality of time
and how it relates to eternity, the Holy One, and our own
living experience. However, trying to understand time is
only part of the challenge. Harry Emerson Fosdick once ob
served that we can put off making up our minds, but we can
not put off making up our lives. We have to decide concrete
ly even when we do not comprehend perfectly, and so the
other facet of challenge is learning living with the mysteri
ous reality of time and all that it does to the world and
ourselves.

The author approaches both the intellectual and practi
cal challenges by asking directly: "Is time a friend or an ene
my?" He then very honestly struggles with the many facets
of such an inquiry. I appreciate his honesty. He does not at
tempt to evade complexity or try to make simple what is in
fact full of density. He shares both his knowledge and feel
ings with the reader, and this constitutes an act of high gen
erosity. If one tells me only what he or she knows or thinks,
that is one thing. To be allowed in on the struggles of the
soul and the multifaceted feelings that accompany struggle
is even more enriching, because it gives me permission to be
honest about my dilemmas and uncertainties as well as em
bracing new insights.

Reading this author's "arm wrestle" with this primal re
ality made me aware that he is doing what every human has

to do with the whole of reality, and that is to find a way to come to terms with God and relate that to our individual preferences and desires. Reading these pages reminded me of the passage out of Nikos Kanzautzakis' book, *Report to Greco*. It seems that a young religious seeker made his way to the strip of land on the coast of Greece known as Mount Athos, where over a millennia holy men and hermits of all stripes have lived in isolation and sought to know the deepest truth about the Ultimate One. The young man asked a wise old hermit: "Father, do you still wrestle with the devil?"

"Oh, no," replied the holy man, "I'm too old for that. I wrestle now with God."

The young man's eyes widened with wonder, and he exclaimed, "With God! Do you hope to win?"

"Oh, no, my son, I hope to lose," said the hermit.

I think this would be where Al Cadenhead hopes to come out as well. As utterly mysterious and sometimes obscure as God's ways appear, the way to win is to relinquish our less than perfect perceptions to God. Losing to God is the final victory indeed! This is where I see the author ending in his struggles with the reality of time.

JOHN R. CLAYPOOL

ACKNOWLEDGMENTS

A book is never the product of one person. Even if the pen never changes hands, the influence of so many people is clear. I offer thanks to the church office staff, Wyanne Hall and Truellen Baker, for their constant assistance, always with a smile. I am personally indebted to family and friends for support and encouragement, during the many months of this writing. I would be negligent if I did not express my gratitude to the congregation of The Hill Baptist Church for not only allowing my writing ministry but prayerfully supporting it. They are special people, and I thank God for them. To Suzanne, who constantly endures with no criticism about the late night lights from the study, thanks.

INTRODUCTION

I s time a friend or an enemy? The answer that you give to this question is very important. Your answer will influence your life mentally, emotionally, physiologically, and spiritually. If time is your friend, there will be a sense of peace that characterizes your perception of time. If time is an enemy, life takes on the landscape of a battleground. Struggles are to be expected in life; but it seems to me that some battles should be avoided.

Is time a friend or an enemy? Something within me makes me feel like I should say, "Yes, of course time is my friend!" But, if I am really candid, I must confess that, "I am just not so sure." The core of my trouble is that there are some characteristics of time which I do not like. Consider what time does to our bodies. I do not always like the changes that occur. Bodies, once young and agile, become stiff and fragile. Bodies which once would have played in the rain now dread damp weather as a source of pain for old bones.

I do not like what time does to special places. There was a large wooded area close to my house, when I was a boy. Those woods were a special place. The combination of the forest and boyhood imagination filled those woods with priceless experiences. Those woods are not there any longer. We fought wars in those woods. We marched with Davy Crockett, Robert E. Lee, and General McArthur in those woods. Those few acres were as big as the universe. They were sacred and full of mystery at the same time.

But, they are not there any longer. A street with sidewalks and street lights now is there instead. I have nothing against streets, but the secrets of those woods are lost forever. Children can ride their bicycles on the sidewalks, but they will never raise the flag from their fort and fight a foreign army, enemy aircraft, or tank. They cannot share a tree hut with a dog named Clem who was afraid of heights. Why? Time is the reason for all the changes.

Many of the other changes that time brings upon us are much more significant than just the loss of a particular forest that we really didn't own anyway. Other influences of time are of life threatening significance.

The words offered in the pages that follow are not words of a poet, philosopher, or historian. They are simply the observations and confessions of a man who suddenly finds himself dealing with time, not because he necessarily wants to but because the swift passing of time has left him no choice.

I must also say that my uninvited struggle with time has become a matter of faith. Time is not external to God's working in my life. In fact, in the course of this journey I have discovered that time belongs to God and time becomes one of the primary means of God's touch upon my life and journey. My perception and understanding of time is directly related to my perception and understanding of God. Therefore, my concern with time has become a religious quest and very personal one!

Even the writing of this book has been a case study of time. The following pages were written over a period of eighteen months. During that time, I spent a lot more time carrying my briefcase than I did opening it and working out of it. The primary reason was an issue of time, or shall I say "the lack of it." I have put thousands of miles on my briefcase so that I might feel better about the deadline that would inevitably come. The deadline did come and Al was not ready. My editor was his usual understanding self and gave me four more months. I put some more miles on my briefcase and managed to send the manuscript in just under the wire.

During the months of carrying my briefcase around so much has happened in my life. I might add that there were no significant crises. The events were generally routine, predictable, and expected. Adjustment and change are our constant companions in life. The last few months have been a perfect opportunity for me to seriously come to terms with my perception of time.

In the earlier pages of this book, I am dealing with some expected events in the life of any parent—the anticipated departure of my son for college and the entrance of my daughter into the "roller coaster ride" of adolescence. Yet, my struggle with time goes far beyond these anticipated adjustments. The pages that follow are primarily confessional. During the days of writing, I have not only learned a few things about time but have actually changed my attitude about and perception of time. The journey has been a learning experience for me.

I must also confess that the end did not turn out as I expected. I really anticipated that I would give to you all kinds of "how to's" so that time would become a friendlier companion to you. The reperceiving that took place in my own life was at a much deeper level and could not be related by giving some quick "how to" advice. What I discovered even surprised me.

Changing one's perception of time from the status of enemy to that of a friend is no easy task. One cannot take a passive attitude. Such a change in attitude requires an intentional effort to make friends with one of God's great gifts to us.

If you are looking for a distinctly intellectually and historically philosophical presentation of time, you are wasting your time and whatever you paid for this book. If you are interested in the sharing of a man's heart as he struggles with the swift passing of time, then read on. A little time will be required. "But this I say, brethen, the time is short" (1 Cor. 7:29, KJV).

> I sometimes feel the thread of life is slender,
> And soon with me the labor will be wrought;
> Then grows my heart to other hearts more tender.
> The time is short.
>
> —D. M. Craik

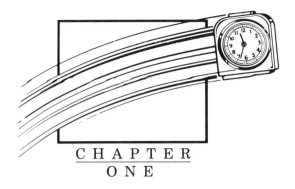

The Swift Passing of Time

"The race is on and here comes pride. . . ."

T hese past few years have been difficult ones for me. In a very short period of time a number of events in my life have really affirmed for me the fact that time is marching on. At times I have felt as though it were marching right over me. I can only speak for myself when I say that moving into the "forties" was tough. If you have not arrived there yet, don't become apprehensive based on my experience. If you have already journeyed through this wilderness experience, you may have found no struggle. For me it has been a long series of little things. For example, it was the period of time when my son became driving age and received this symbol of adolescent freedom—his driver's license. He no longer needed old pop to chauffeur him. In fact, old pop began to feel like he was in the way.

Simultaneously my daughter, whom I subconsciously assumed would always be a little girl, began to go through some very normal changes that indicated she was growing up. On one hand I would not have it any other way, and yet I also liked having a *little* girl around.

One day during that same period of time, my hairdresser said she had decided not to charge me full price for cutting my hair, since it was taking her less time. Out of vain pride I

17

told her either she would charge me full price or I would find another miracle worker who was not so courteous.

It was also within that same time frame that I employed a secretary whose parents were younger than I am. I reassured myself by believing that they gave birth to her when they were nine years of age. Another blow came to my old prideful soul when my ophthalmologist wrote out the prescription for reading glasses in addition to increasing the strength of regular lenses. Young men don't wear bifocals. The truth hurts!

I solved the bifocal problem by just using two pair of glasses—one regular pair and one reading pair. The problem is that in the pulpit I am constantly swapping glasses. Doing so has helped to keep my congregation awake and on their toes. Several people have expressed concern that they are afraid that someday I am going to try to put both of them on at the same time. Prayers become an excellent time for swapping glasses so that no one notices. I have discovered that I am praying more and more throughout my sermons.

I also found myself doing some rather interesting things. I traded my comfortable, traditional, preacher-type Olds Ninety-eight for a twenty-five year old Mustang with "glasspack" mufflers. Then I began to get the attention of some other people, including some of my deacons. They laughed and accused me of going through a mid-life crisis. One deacon, in jest, commented that it was obvious that I was dealing with mid-life and that he was glad that I had chosen old cars as my method instead of young women. I just laughed and pretended as though I didn't know what he was talking about.

The Truth Hurts

Truthfully, I knew exactly what my deacon friend was joking about. I had assumed that the notorious mid-life crisis was for uniformed people. After all, I have a degree in counseling and have worked in a counseling role for many years with lots of people who were dealing with this rather expected stage of life. I had made up my mind long ago that if I had any hair left when the time came, I was not going to get a curly permanent nor a big gold chain for my neck and would make my entrance into middle age with dignity and grace.

I expected a lot of these things to happen to me physically, but I really was not ready for what the changes of time would do to things all around me. My world was changing faster than I wanted to admit and accept.

I will confess that much of what I was experiencing was the result of a predictable, normal, mid-life crisis. The symptoms and feelings were right out of the textbook. But I believe more is involved than just turning forty. I truly sense the workings of God in my life to come to terms with time. Time is an issue of tremendous importance. To deny such an important reality is to deny life itself. To deny the relevance of time results only in weakness, fear, and unnecessary distance from God.

When I was a boy, the swift passing of time was not a problem, at least with a few exceptions. Do you remember the childlike anticipation of Christmas? Many years seemed to pass between each Christmas Day. For months and months I would long for Christmas to arrive. I really felt like it was within reach when the Sears Christmas catalog arrived. As I waited, I counted the days, marked them off on the calendar, and imagined what Christmas Day would bring.

The days just prior to Christmas seemed like months as they passed. Then Christmas Day would arrive and the excitement was indescribable. As the day began to pass I would realize that it was over for all practical purposes. Now I could only look forward to next year. Like every other child I wanted Christmas Day to last forever. I was not interested only in the gifts but the "magical spell" of the day.

I can remember a routine that I would go through in the evening of every Christmas Day. In order to slow the depressing descent from the emotional orbit, I would go through a rather silly process of convincing myself that it was Christmas night, rather than Christmas Eve, that was important anyway. After all, Jesus was born on Christmas Day and not Christmas Eve and the celebrating ought to be done on the evening of Christmas Day. Yet, I could remember the excitement of the night before and the sparkle of Christmas morning which now seemed another world away. In order to prolong the excitement, however, I would make a desperate attempt to feel excited about Christmas evening. The more I tried to stretch the day, the faster it seemed to go by.

I recall two impressions especially about the day after Christmas. First, my mother had the tree undecorated and out on the street by dawn. Second, a Christmas of next year may as well have been a century away. There was a deep sense of sadness as the day of all days became a memory. The time mode changed again. The light speed of Christmas Day changed to slow motion as we looked toward next year. The fifty-two weeks between Christmas celebrations seemed like an eternity.

Childhood Anticipation

Time meant very little to me as a boy. If anything, time got in the way. A child lives in anticipation, the magic of childhood. The great philosopher Charles Schultz was right on target when his cartoon character Charlie Brown once defined *happiness* as, "Having three things to look forward to and nothing to dread."

Upon the completion of one experience a child is anticipating the next. Such a habit is not a flaw of childhood. In fact, far from being a flaw, it is one of the secrets of joy. It is one of God's gracious gifts. Sad is the fact that in adulthood we loose that sense of anticipation. A sense of expectancy should never be just a childhood characteristic.

I remember as a boy the anticipation of our family's annual vacation. A brief trip to the beach was always worked into the budget, and we looked forward to it from one year to the next. We would always leave very early in the morning so that we could be there by dawn and have the advantage of another full day without the extra motel bill.

Vacations were not vacations unless you went to the beach. They did not count unless you returned home with sand in everything. We traveled with anticipation, and the minute we saw the ocean the time mode changed from slow to light speed. Those few days would fly by! We had hardly gotten there when it was time to pack up and head back for home.

I can remember even now that every year, as we drove away, my sister and I would ask my dad if there was a chance we could make a quick trip back to the beach before cold weather, affirming Charlie Brown's theory that a part of happiness is having something to look forward to. My dad would always say, "maybe." We always knew the truth, that there was neither time nor money. However, there was next year; and, even though the time mode changed once again to slow motion, we could look forward to next year's vacation. But next year's journey seemed a hundred years away.

The problem now is that the time mode no longer changes back and forth from slow to fast. Time for me is hung on fast speed. I've tried every gimmick known to slow it down, but it continues to march on at an incredibly fast pace and actually seems to pick up speed.

The Struggle
with Time

"The tide moves in and out."

The tradition of beach trips continues today in my own family. We recently made our annual pilgrimage to the land of sand and sunburn; and, as they say in the social section of the newspaper, "a good time was had by all." How I wish I could freeze those moments when the family is together and everyone is healthy, happy, and carefree. The laughter is always the best part. Long after everything else, I remember the laughter. It isn't programmed. It just happens.

Laughter is a special gift from God that most of us have never developed. It is free; and, when taken in right proportions, it is a touch of the divine upon our troubled souls. You cannot laugh and worry at the same time. Anyway, back to the beach.

On one of our days on the beach my daughter, Melody, decided to construct a sand castle. I must concede that she worked quite diligently. I wanted to help so I supervised from under the umbrella, in between naps. Earlier in the day her brother, in a weak moment, had bought her a sand bucket that also doubled as a mold for a castle tower. Vacations are intriguing. They cause people to do things otherwise thought impossible. The sand bucket is a perfect example. After all, even big brothers have their compassionate moments, especially at the beach. Or was it that he was desperate for any excuse to get the car keys and get away from boring parents? I think I know the truth. He even paid for the bucket, a cheap price for the cause of freedom.

Melody built a masterpiece of a castle. King Arthur would have been proud to live in such an environment. She also built it high on the beach to avoid the tide as long as possible. The day was an experience of simple pleasure with a price tag far beyond dollars.

The beach walkers were courteous as they stepped over the castle. Some even offered compliments on her handiwork. There were several people pitching a ball who made great efforts to avoid the area. The sand castle seemed to be protected from all of the hazards of a busy beach, which is an interesting world in and of itself. All appeared safe as I sat in my beach chair and stood guard over Melody's sandy kingdom. A problem began to develop.

As the afternoon passed, the tide began to inch its way over the sand and toward the castle. Time was bringing impending change. Melody tried to position a plastic raft in front of the castle as she tried to shield it against the encroaching waves. Slowly but surely the waves worked their way around the area and soon began to erase in only a few minutes what Melody had spent the better part of the day building and protecting.

I watched the waves do their work and soon the castle no longer existed. I felt sad. It was just a castle, but not any castle. Melody had made it.

And yet there was nothing evil about what had taken place. The waves washing upon the beach were a natural part of the day. Time called for the tide to move in and out, and no amount of protecting would prevent the washing away of a sand castle. The castle was to be enjoyed for a while and then given back to the sea. Fight the waves as much as you please, but their course remains the same.

Time Is Not Evil

In a very practical way the same can be said about time. It is not evil. Time is just time and does its work as a natural part of God's plan. One can struggle against time and even lash out in anger against it, but time continues right along with the tide moving in and out.

At this point in my life I must be honest and confess that I am having great difficulty accepting the natural movement of time. Never before in my life have I tried harder to slow the hands of time than during recent days. It moves so fast. Weeks go by like days. Days are over before they hardly begin. And who can even keep up with hours anymore?

I honestly want to perceive time as a friend and realize that such a perspective is the only attitude that makes any sense at all. Yet, so much around me is changing that my inclination is to declare war on time as an enemy.

Does time really have to be an enemy? Something within me says that life would be sweeter if I could get to the point where time was counted as a friend. If it is such a natural thing within the province of God, then it couldn't be evil. And how do you declare war on something that does not even acknowledge your declaration of war? Time takes it's course absolutely unaltered by the frantic efforts of combat.

Learning from the Past

I should be able to learn from past experiences that time is not always seeking to do me in. Allow me to give one example that is current. Watching my family grow older causes mixed feelings, both intensely painful and tremendously joyful. I can remember when my children were small, and I would periodically become despondent when I realized they were growing out of some particular stage. They would move from diapers to the mobile stage, from shy stages to bold stages, or from babyish ways to older ways. I would think to myself that no stage could ever be as intriguing as the current one. I would feel sad as that stage began to melt away. But, the next stage was just as exciting. That same process still continues on today.

My once, little boy, who would usually do a cute, innocent dance when I came home each evening, is now six feet tall with bigger feet, a bigger heart, and a bigger brain than his dad. We are closer than ever, even though time has altered that cute innocent image that lingers in my mind to this day.

During this past year, his mother and I have had to say good-bye to him as he left home for college. How can that be possible? It seems that only a few months have passed since he was a little boy! Most of us live as though our children will always be around. We have all kinds of plans, so many things we shall do together. Then in just a matter of moments they are grown. We turn around once and everything has changed. Where has the time gone?

There is an obvious lesson here for me, if I could remove my emotional blinders long enough. I should let the lessons from those earlier stages teach me about the outcome of this one. I need to remember that, in the past, the next stage of my children was more exciting than the previous one. Why can I not accept the same truth about a child leaving home for college?

Incidentally, Joseph Bayly in a beautifully written book entitled *The Last Things We Talk About* shares an observation that I find very helpful. He is speaking of the death of a child, but what he says can be applied to other times in life when we are experiencing what appears to be loss. He says, "We don't own our children; we hold them in trust for God, who gave them to us. The eighteen or twenty years of provision and oversight and training that we normally have, represent our fulfillment of that trust."[1]

It seems to me that the struggle to slow time down only

serves to speed it up even more. A more logical approach would be to take a more open and receptive stance toward time, although such an attitude is more easily talked about than lived out in daily life.

Not All Bad

Consider the good things that time does. At the risk of sounding like Dear Abby let me give another personal example. I think of my wife of twenty-one years. I can learn a lesson from that experience as well. She is not the same person I married. Twenty-one years has done a lot to both of us. My memory of those early years is a gift from God, a possession no one can steal. We do not necessarily relate like we did then. We do not even look like we did then, at least she doesn't. Even though I may look the same; let's face it, she looks a little older! Why? Time. But, I must be honest about something. At the risk of sounding like a melancholy romantic I must admit that if I had a choice of her then or her now, I would choose her now. Why? Because time has done good things to her.

The point I am trying to make is simple. I want time to be my friend. I do not want to struggle with it in such a frustrating and exhausting way as I have in the past. Developing new attitudes about time may be one of life's greatest challenges. The issue of time is certainly not foreign to the Bible. The writer of Ecclesiastes reminds us, "To everything there is a season, A time for every purpose under heaven" (Eccl. 3:1). Time is a gift from God, not a curse. Time is granted like all good gifts, beyond our deserving. Like all gifts we must be wise enough to graciously receive that which comes from the Father.

Thomas Carlyle long ago wrote:

> So here hath been dawning another blue day;

The Struggle with Time

Think, wilt thou let it slip useless away?
Out of eternity this new day is born;
Into eternity at night will return.

The Bible has so much to say about time, particularly its purpose "under Heaven." This gift from God is a part of His plan. His purpose is bound up in the movement of time.

Jesus compared the Kingdom to the sowing of seed. Time would then bring about His plan. "First the blade, then the head, after that the full grain in the head" (Mark 4:28). There is no random, accidental nature to time. Time is directly bound up in God's work. There is movement, purpose, and significance.

In the nineteenth century Anna Waring wrote:

I love to think that God appoints
My portion day by day;
Events of life are in His hand,
And I would only say,
Appoint them in Thine own good time,
And in Thine own best way.

One issue is clear to me. I want to ease my struggle with time. I want to change its status from enemy to friend. If time is bound up in God's plan, am I stretching the point too far to assume that in struggling with time I am therefore struggling with God? Such a feeling makes me very uncomfortable. There must be another way.

Note

1. Joseph Bayly, *The Last Thing We Talk About* (Elgin, Ill.: Cook Publishing Co., 1973), 67.

Measuring Time

"Starlight, starbright, first star I've seen . . ."

O ut of curiosity I asked a number of people, "Tell me what comes to your mind when you hear the word *time*." The question was intentionally nonspecific so that I might hear their initial associations with and impressions about time. As one might expect, most of the responses fell into two main categories. One immediate association for the majority of people with the word *time* was concerning the shortage of time. "There is just never enough time to get it all done! If every day just had a few more hours in it." Certainly, most of us can identify with the pressing sense of demand under which most of us live.

The second category into which the responses fell was that of clocks and watches. For many the initial association with the word was in terms of measurement. Our culture is obsessed with "keeping track" of time. We have time pieces that range from the simple wind up watch to the sophisticated chronometer that can tell you what time it is in fifty-six countries at any given moment. Hey, my life hangs in suspense waiting for that kind of information!

Those of us who really want to change the status of time from enemy to friend must look beneath the surface issues of time. The answer is not to be found in more refined and sophisticated ways of measuring this mysterious creation of God. We should be able to learn that lesson from just a brief look at the history of humankind's struggle with time.

28

Time is one of the deepest mysteries known to human beings. Yet, most of our energies have been used in trying to measure it. We have to acknowledge that the ability to measure time makes our way of life possible. Our life depends upon doing things at the right time. The results would be total chaos, if we did not have a uniform way of measuring time. Without a consistent and accepted method, life would be unimaginable.

Just think about the people who crowd Times Square each year to watch the big apple drop on New Year's Eve. Without some kind of uniform measurement of time they would have to stay there all year just to experience the thrill of watching that ridiculous ritual! By the way, I feel certain that there is some hidden meaning in that experience that has thus far eluded me. A million people crowded into one city block is not my idea of pleasant company or a relaxed evening on the town. I have thus far been denied that experience, but life must go on.

Nevertheless, since the beginning of time humans have sought the best way to measure this mysterious entity called time. These measurements were usually based on clearly recognizable changes that take place.

Two Kinds of Changes

There are two kinds of changes—those that happen only once and those that happen over and over again. A change that takes place again and again stands out from other changes that occur only once. A tree in the forest falls only once, but the sun passes overhead everyday.

There is an interesting phenomenon that has become apparent at this point. Those changes that occurred over and over again on a regular basis became the measure for changes that occurred only once. The time of the falling tree was placed against the measure of the moving sun. Thus, time and change are related because the measurement of time depends on changes taking place. In the real world, changes never stop taking place.

For early civilizations the most obvious regular changes were the motions of objects in the sky. After all, what else could they do at night? They had no television, computer games, or shopping malls. They had little else to do before they went to sleep, except notice the endless array of lights that filled the dark sky above.

The most obvious of these repeated changes was the rising and setting of the sun. While primitive humans could not explain this mysterious body of heat and power, humans quickly learned that their existence depended on it. Each of these cycles of the sun came to be called a day.

The moon became another object of intrigue. What a mysterious body! It always seemed to be changing shapes. Then people began to notice a rhythm to the changing shapes. Each cycle of this strange body's changing shape took about twenty-nine and one half days and came to be known as a month.

Humans noticed the regularity of things on the earth growing and dying. The change of the seasons gave people a valuable tool for measuring time. At first there may have been some question as to whether the sun or the earth was doing the cycling. They observed that the cycle required 365¼ days and came to be known as a year.

For a long, long time people tried to fit days and months evenly into a year or period of years. Nothing worked well. Finally the calendar was based entirely upon the measure of a year. Even though the year is divided into the familiar twelve months, the months have no relation to the actual cycle of the moon.

We did not create our seven-day period by looking into the sky. To oversimplify, the seven-day week came from the Jewish custom of observing the sabbath every seventh day. The hours, minutes, and seconds probably came from the

Babylonians, who were interested in astrology. They divided the path of the sun into twelve equal parts. Then they divided the periods of daylight and darkness into twelve parts each, and the result was a twenty-four hour day.

The Sun, the Ancient "Time Piece"

The ancient Babylonians also are accredited with dividing the path of the sun into 360 degrees. Then the hours were divided into sixty minutes and then into seconds. Directly above every spot on the earth there is an imaginary curved line called the celestial meridian. As the earth rotates on its axis, the sun crosses every celestial meridian once each day. The time at that point is called noon. Twelve hours later is called midnight. This period of time from midnight to the next is called a solar day.

To make all solar days the same length, astronomers do not measure solar time with the real sun. They use an imaginary average sun that moves at a steady speed around the sky. Mean solar moon occurs when the mean sun crosses the celestial meridian above a particular place. The time between one mean solar moon and the next is always the same length.

Our methods of measuring time are so inexact. For example, astronomers also measure time by the earth's rotation in relation to the stars. This method of measurement is called sidereal time. As the earth rotates on its axis an imaginary point among the stars called the vernal equinox crosses the celestial meridian above every place on the earth. When this happens, the time is sidereal noon. The reason I mention this method is that a sidereal day is three minutes and fifty-six seconds shorter than a mean solar day. Does that mean that time is different between the two methods? No, the difference is strictly a matter of measurement.

If you are still with me, I offer my thanks. There is a point to this. Stay with me.

Time, Independent of Its Measure

The intriguing thing to me is that these regular changes became the basis for measuring irregular changes. Change measuring change. There must be some kind of moral or lesson to that realization, especially for those of us who perceive change as alien and evil. Life absolutely hangs on change. Change becomes our way of perceiving life and measuring it. The Greek philosopher, Heraclitus, has wisely pointed out that, "One cannot step into the same river twice." His point was obvious. The world is constantly changing. In fact, our world hangs on change. We will talk more about change in another chapter.

We have difficulty thinking of time in any way other than a fundamental quantity that can be measured, such as weight and mass. Time, however, is never governed by our ways of measuring it and is never affected by our units of measure but continues even in the absence of measurement.

Just when we think our method is precise and accurate, someone comes along and points out that our measure is filled with flaws. For example, Albert Einstein realized that time was affected by motion. According to his theory of relativity, time as we understand it is affected by gravity and light. If his theory is true, matter cannot be transported faster than the speed of light without the matter being destroyed. If we moved faster than the speed of light we would theoretically cease to exist.

My mind goes into shock when I carry this theory out to one particular conclusion. If time is affected by gravity and light, what happens to time within a black hole. A *black hole* is a phenomenon of outer space. It is a collapsed star or even a collapsed galaxy due to an overwhelming force of gravity. *Gravity* is result of mass; and because the gravity is so great, light cannot penetrate the black hole. If light cannot penetrate, then theoretically time no longer exists. Such a thought baffles my meager brain.

My point, nevertheless, remains that time is not subject to our meager methods of measurement. Our methods may have progressed from the sundial to the hourglass to the water clock to the electronic clock to the atomic clock, but they are all deficient methods of measuring something that is totally independent of our attempts to control.

Time and Its Unchanged Speed

I, along with countless others, have made the statement that time seems to move so much faster as we get older. Weeks pass like days now. When we were children, time just didn't move so quickly. The truth is that time has never changed its speed. It passes no faster now than it did one hundred years ago. And to be honest it has nothing to do with the way we measure it. Our sophisticated time pieces have changed nothing about time.

The congregation I serve is a very affirming and caring group of people. They recently gave Suzanne and me a surprise appreciation dinner. Among the gifts to me was a beautiful watch. It is something I will always treasure, not just because it is an expensive piece of jewelry but because of its source. One might be tempted to think that a watch which costs much money would have some kind of influence on the time of its wearer. But the truth is that I have no more time in my day than if I wore a watch that came from the local convenient store at a price of ninety-five cents. The only thing that has changed is that several members have threatened to take it back, if I don't learn how to recognize noon on Sunday.

To extend or diminish time is not our option, only to use it more wisely. More accurate measurement is not the answer to our dilemma. When we embrace time as a gift from God and a treasure beyond measure, then we are on track. Benjamin Franklin once said, "Dost thou love life? Then waste not time for time is the stuff life is made of."

Time is life, and life is never subject to a watch. The watch may stop, and it eventually will; but time as we know it now goes right on, absolutely unhindered. However, there will come a day when "time shall be no more." We'll talk about that later in the book, provided there is time.

Time: According to the Bible

"Round and round she goes. Where she stops . . ."

Y ou and I are certainly not the first to try to come to
terms about the nature of time. There have been many
before us who have wrestled with the same questions that
we raise. For example, what is time anyway? When did it
begin? Does it have an end? And if so, what happens then? Is
time really going somewhere? Does it move in cycles or a
straight line or in various directions like a stream flowing
down a hillside? Are we a part of time, or is time a part of
us?

Does time occur within us or without? Is it a product of
our imagination? The eighteenth century philosopher Im-
manuel Kant believed that space and time exist within our
consciousness. For one like Kant, time is more of a subjective than an objective reality. Kant would argue that time
and space must be subjective. Otherwise, it would run out.
And what happens when time and space run out? Is more
out there somewhere else?

The intriguing irony of this mystery is that we think we
understand time until we try to explain it. I feel like I know
exactly what time is until I try to describe it in words. As
soon as I try to communicate my perception of time I become dumbfounded with no words that impart what I am
thinking.

Men and women of all ages have sought answers to similar questions and one must assume that very few satisfactory answers have been found. To be perfectly honest, I find very little comfort in the fact that I am not the first who has sought to "put a handle" on time and with little apparent success. If time is to be a friend instead of an enemy, I must have a better idea of what time really is. After all, it is usually easier to be friends with someone when you know more about that person. In personal relationships I can usually be more understanding and sympathetic when I know someone personally. If it applies to other relationships, then maybe it would apply to time as well.

The struggle has been going on for a long time. For example, the Mesopotamians and the Babylonians were among the first to make serious attempts to unscramble the mystery of time. But, once again as with others who would follow, most of their energies were spent by trying to measure this elusive dynamic of life.

Many of the ancient cultures, especially the Greeks, believed that time moved in a circle. They believed that the events of time would repeat themselves. This circular concept of time explains why so many of the earlier cultures believed in reincarnation. Such a belief would be a natural outgrowth of a cyclical understanding of history, that time goes nowhere. It only repeats itself over and over. Such a perception of time takes on the role of a prison. One is caught up in an endless cycle that operates like a trap. One cannot get out, and the best hope is only that next time around things will be better.

The impact of Old Testament thinking concerning time is unquestioned. The Hebrew concept of time and history was nothing less than revolutionary. Against a world that envisioned time as moving in a circle, the Hebrews believed that history had purpose and was moving in a definite direction.

The purpose of time and history was the revelation of Yahweh their God. God was working through history and seeking to fulfill Himself in the course of time. Time was not an unvarying, repetitive cycle of events. It had a purpose as well as direction. History was an instrument of the living God as He sought to reveal Himself and His plan for the human race.

Yet, even the Old Testament bears the influence of the Greek perception of the circular movement of time. The most obvious was the writer of the book of Ecclesiastes. There are as many interpretations of Ecclesiastes as there are commentators. The writer of Ecclesiastes has been identified as various characters, including Solomon in his latter years.

Words of a Frustrated Man

Regardless of who wrote the book, most of his words convey the thoughts of a frustrated and disillusioned man, at least in the initial chapters of the book. One of the concerns of the writer of Ecclesiastes is the issue of time. The author, known in Hebrew as Koheleth and frequently just called the preacher, is trying to deal with the fear of growing old and dying without ever feeling that he had actually been alive.

Some scholars have suggested that he seems to be a bitter man who is quite cynical about the orthodoxy of his day. He is past the midpoint in his life. Lots of thoughts whirl around in his thinking. Deep within Koheleth's voice there is a sense of terror. He is truly a frightened man, afraid that he will die before he has learned how to live. Nothing he has ever done will amount to anything. He will die someday, and it will be as if he had never lived.

Listen to the feelings behind the words:
"As it happens to the fool,
It also happens to me,

And why was I then more wise?"
Then I said in my heart,
"This also is vanity."
For there is no more remembrance of
the wise than of the fool forever,
Since all that now is will be forgotten
in the days to come (Eccl. 2:15-16).

Koheleth (the preacher) describes life through a series of antitheses. These contrasting antitheses form the background for our existence. There is a time to be born and a time to die, a time to plant and a time to take up that which was planted, a time to weep and a time to laugh, and a time to mourn and a time to dance. The list goes on. These predictable conditions in life are the best one can hope for.

Harold Kushner in his book, *When All You've Ever Wanted Isn't Enough*, says of Ecclesiastes, "Time, which was once the source of his advantage over older people, has now become his enemy. He is starting to realize that he is running out of time."[1]

Koheleth believes that the course of nature does not alter itself. The present is as the past; nothing is new, and this routine is the totality of a human's existence. He believes in his heart that life leads to no lasting gain. Does time accomplish anything? Koheleth has tested, and tested, and concluded that there is no real gain. He has occupied himself with great enterprises, built apparent monuments, and amassed great wealth. He has developed his mind and become wise. But, in the end a wise man dies just like the fool (Eccl. 2:16).

A process of opposites is perceived in the human situation. There is life and death, doing and not doing, and weeping and laughing. There is a season for all things. Yet this is not perceived as freedom but perplexity. Life is just an eternal round of opposites. "That which is has already been, And what is to be has already been" (3:15)

These contrasting antitheses become a trap for Ecclesiastes. They become rigid boundaries for life and they are the best one can hope for. For this frustrated man, the regularity of the processes of nature could no longer be perceived as positive but rather bringing to surface in the human heart the feeling of weariness, disappointment, and despair. Koheleth tried wealth, works, wisdom, and religion to give meaning to his life. Nothing seemed to work. This depressing nature comes from a cyclical understanding of time and history. Ecclesiastes has a Greek perception of time, not Hebrew.

In all fairness this ancient writer, in his own despairing way, said that nothing can fill the God-shaped void in a human being's life but God Himself. He encouraged one to seek God early in life. "Remember now your Creator in the days of your youth, Before the difficult days come" (Eccl. 12:1). In spite of it all one should fear God and keep His commandments.

I place Koheleth in the spotlight because most of the book attributed to him is descriptive of the attitudes of people today. They could care less whether their thought is of Greek or Hebrew origin. They just know that they feel trapped by life. Life does not seem to be going anywhere. It is just one long series of opposites that form a great wall around human life. For some it is the trap of poverty. For others the prison comes in the form of culture, social barriers, or family burdens. For many it is the hopeless future of a meaningless job.

Koheleth's perception of life and time did not disappear in his "day." The plague of meaningless existence is at epidemic proportions today. Too many people feel caught by life rather than experiencing a sense of joy in life. The sun may shine today, but it will rain tomorrow. Life is lived between the two opposites. Does one have a right to expect anything more in life?

There is an unquestionable rhythm to life, one that adds predictability to our days. There is a time to plant and a time to reap, a time to laugh and a time to cry, and a time to grieve and a time to celebrate. But life is not a cyclical prison that traps people inside a clothes dryer with only the next cycle to anticipate.

The Prophets

The influence of the Old Testament is very refreshing as one hears how God works through time. The prophets, especially Isaiah, repeatedly reminded their hearers that the God of Israel is the ruler of time. On the human side, faith, born in the encounter with the God of the future, carries the conviction that something new has appeared in history. In the case of Abraham this is obvious. Although he would never see its actualization, Israel came into existence in him. Israel's starting point was his act of faith in a God who worked through time and history.

History for the Hebrew was never accidental or incidental. History became the vehicle for the God who called it all into being in the beginning. History always had significance. Time was the possession of the living God and the future could be approached with anticipation.

Abraham's starting point was his act of faith. While he could not look beyond the curtain of the years to Sinai, Calvary, and the long record of the triumphs and disasters of the Christian church, his act of faith in the God of time set in motion a direction that is called revelation.

Richard Toombs in his book, *The Old Testament In Christian Preaching*, says,

> This conviction of Abraham has a vital message for the contemporary world where people are so often oppressed by the meaninglessness of life. Whenever God touches a person, in that moment something new and significant begins. A train of events is set in motion by the act of faith, of which

the end result can neither be seen nor predicted, but which has permanent meaning in the purpose of God.[2]

In other words, there is a sense of direction to the movement of time. It has meaning that comes from the fact that God is using history to bring about His ultimate will. Time is not accidental or incidental. It is not a repetitive cycle that goes nowhere and means only what one experiences at that given moment.

Faith opens up the long view and reveals the far horizon, because it lifts the isolated, mortal human being out of hopelessness and meaninglessness and makes him or her a part of the ongoing purpose of the God of all eternity.

Expansion of Time

If the Old Testament gives time a sense of movement and direction, the New Testament places it within the context of eternity. Due to the teachings of Jesus, time has been expanded beyond the limits of the Old Testament. In fact, nothing has ever influenced our perception of time more than the incarnation, whether we are aware of that fact or not.

The New Testament does not intentionally seek to provide a well organized study of time. The nature and meaning of time is not an issue as such. The impact comes in a secondary way, in the process of declaring and defining the incarnation.

The issue of time surfaces as a result of another question. Some passages seem to teach that at death one is immediately presented with a risen body. Other passages seem to teach that these bodies are to be given at the time of Jesus' coming.

Does this mean that there is a contradiction in the New Testament? Absolutely not! However, in order to bring these two views together one must take a "short course" in the theology of time. The bottom line is that what appears to be an interval of time to us is no interval at all to God (or those who have entered into life with Him because of death).

The writer of 2 Peter says, "But, beloved, do not forget this one thing, that with the Lord one day is as a thousand years, and a thousand years as one day" (3:8). Is that just a biblical way of saying that the Lord is unaffected by time? In one sense, yes, but so much more is implied in those few words. We can go as far as to say that time is not even a factor in eternity. Time is found within eternity, but eternity is qualitatively different from time. Eternity transcends time.

The Bible makes it clear that Christ is the same yesterday, today, and tomorrow. Does this mean that He has some kind of special protective garment that allows Him to throw aside the influences of time that affect us minute by minute? No. Christ who is the beginning and the end transcends time. He is beyond it. He is related to time only in the sense that, "The Word became flesh and dwelt among us, and we beheld His glory" (John 1:14). History is that period within which the eternal has revealed itself. That which is totally beyond time became history so that history might become a part of eternity.

A Beginning and an End

History has a beginning and an end. Eternity does not. Because of the fact that "in the fullness of time" Christ entered history from timeless eternity, history is being caught up in the eternal and thus given significance. In Christ, history is brought to fulfillment. Eternity does not just take up where time leaves off. In Christ, the eternal has entered history for a brief moment and thus forever changed the meaning of time.

Dr. Frank Stagg has clearly stated,

God is above time, his "present" not being one which "crumbles away" as the "not yet" becomes the "no longer." Time belongs to creation, but God is the Creator. God is the Lord of time, "for whom the distinctions of time, time-distances, have no significance." For him there is no past or future.[3]

If eternity goes beyond time and is not just an endless succession of it, then there is no difference at death between being with the Lord in a resurrected body now and a body to be presented at the "sound of His coming" at a later date. There is no difference at all. Therefore the Christian is at once with Him and also awaits the resurrection at His coming. What appears to be an interval to us is not an interval outside of history. At death we die to be with the Lord and at the same time await His coming. Past, present, and future are factors only to those of us on this side of the "door" of eternal life.

The great theologian Dr. Emil Brunner has stated it well,

> The date of death differs for each man, for the day of death belongs to this world. Our day of resurrection is the same for all and yet is not separated from the day of death by intervals of centuries—for these time intervals are here, not there in the presence of God, where "a thousand years are as a day."[4]

To quote once again Dr. Frank Stagg, "If this understanding of time and eternity is correct, then it is only to us who are yet within time . . . that the parousia (the Lord's return) and the resurrection are future."[5]

Time becomes a brief set of parentheses within the text of eternity. The past, present, and future belong only to time. They have no relationship to eternity beyond the beginning and end of history as we know it.

Significance for You and Me

To understand time in such a way does not take away the significance of history. We are still accountable for our journey along this moving line. The significance for you and me is that there is so much more beyond what we can categorize as past, present, and future. What we see and touch is not all there is to life. There is life outside the walls of time.

At the very least I am reminded that I do not have to be paranoid about the loss of every passing moment. While minutes can only be spent once, the end suddenly doesn't look quite so awesome. At the very best I can see what is happening to me within the framework of time as but a prelude to something magnificent beyond my current senses.

Time becomes a vehicle in which we all ride for a while. Some may ride longer than others. But there will come a day when the entire road will change. In fact,

> The Lord Himself will descend from heaven with a shout, with the voice of an archangel, and with the trumpet of God. And the dead in Christ will rise first. Then we who are alive and remain shall be caught up together with them in the clouds to meet the Lord in the air. And thus we shall always be with the Lord (1 Thess. 4:16-17).

Time really is not an enemy after all. It is just the process through which the timeless becomes flesh and draws us back to the One in whose image we have been created. We then become timeless as well. I really do like the way that feels!

Notes

1. Harold Kushner, *When All You've Ever Wanted Isn't Enough* (New York: Summit Books, 1986), 39.
2. Richard Toombs, *The Old Testament In Christian Preaching* (Philadelphia: The Westminster Press, 1961), 103.

3. Frank Stagg, *New Testament Theology* (Nashville: Broadman Press, 1962), 330.

4. Emil Brunner, *Eternal Hope* (London: Lutterworth Press, 1954), 152.

5. Stagg, 331.

Submitting to Time

"A wise resignation can . . ."

In an earlier chapter I have already mentioned how the Christmas celebration has became symbolic of my struggle with time. When I was a child, Christmas seemed to take ages to roll around. Decembers were an eternity apart. Since those days, however, something has happened to the calendar. Now Decembers almost follow each other. In fact, my credit card is barely paid off before it is time to use it again.

On the one hand I know that an hour is the same length now as it was a thousand years ago. On the other hand I feel like every passing minute is a little faster than the previous one. I find myself in a definite struggle with time's momentum. And the older I become, the faster it seems to move. It's not so much that I am fearful of getting older nor am I afraid to die. Like most other folks I have a good time at living and would like it to last forever. I know that I must be realistic, however. And thanks to my Lord I know that what I see, feel, and experience now is not all there is.

But I still have to admit that I am uncomfortable with the rapid passing of time. It seems only yesterday that our son was taking his first steps and now he is grown and steps where he chooses. It seems only a few days ago that Suzanne and I were talking about how much we hoped that God would give us a little girl. Now, overnight, she has become a teenager.

The Pace of Time

The harder I try to put on the brakes, the faster time seems to go. Yes, I know time has not changed speeds. But it certainly feels like it. What can we do? How can we slow time down? Let me say only two things at this point.

First, accept reality. Time is something we cannot relive or alter. It marches right on regardless. But, we can change our attitude about it. It helps to remember that time is a gift from God, no more or less than any of His other gifts to us. We are not necessarily entitled to any of it. It comes as a gift.

The second thing we need to remember is that "putting the brakes on time" tends to be a vicious circle. It appears that the more we are aware of its brevity, the more we try to take advantage of it and cram everything we can into our waking hours. The end result is that the increased pace makes it move even faster, and we have only made matters worse. It would help if we could all slow down a bit.

I am not, by any means, suggesting that one take a passive stance toward time. We are not to become victims to this mysterious force called time and conduct our lives as if we are totally at its mercy. Yet, a certain amount of resignation is needful.

As I write this chapter, the section of the country in which I live is going through a significant trauma. A hurricane named Hugo has moved through the Southeast with devastating strength. Beaches, houses, and woodlands have been destroyed by a force too powerful to comprehend. When the sea submits to the force of the wind, the results are beyond belief.

Each summer my family and I have been graciously given

the use of a beachside condominium for our annual vacation. One of the many beautiful distinctives of that spot is a swimming pool that sits between the building and the ocean. It has now been several days since Hugo made his force entry. When the surge came from the hurricane, the gunite pool was completed lifted from the ground and moved twenty feet and left sitting on top of the ground next to the building. The hole where the pool used to be was completely filled with sand, giving no indication that a pool had ever been there.

Sand dunes were completely washed away. The shoreline fence and walkway disappeared totally. At least three feet of sand was washed from the beach itself. The result was that the appearance of the area was drastically changed. That which would normally take a hundred years with the seasonal influence of the ocean was done in only a few hours, an absolutely amazing event. Historic monuments were swept away as if they had never existed. Very little remained the same.

One cannot help but reflect about the impact of the storm on so many people. Certainly no one was effected more than the residents of the hard hit areas. Many of them lost everything. Their homes literally disappeared. There was beach property whose owners finally had the vacation dream house that had long been sought. Many businesses were wiped out. But, the intriguing thing is that the sense of loss was experienced by many, many people in addition to these. There was an overwhelming sense of grief that covered the land far beyond the area which suffered the devastation.

For example, my family owns no property in that region. But, for the last ten years we have taken our family vacations in the Charleston and Myrtle Beach area. Without exception, every place we have stayed has been either destroyed or seriously damaged. None of it will ever be the same. In many ways we, too, feel a sense of loss and grief over what has taken place.

The Force of Time

I have said all of this to lead up to an interesting dynamic of the hurricane. This past summer as we vacationed in Myrtle Beach, residents on more than one occasion made statements that it was time for a "big" hurricane. With no knowledge of weather conditions a lot of people were assuming that it was just time for another "big" one. The only justification for such a prediction was the assumption that time brings about those expected kinds of things. As one woman said, "That's just the way it is."

I never had really associated a hurricane with time. But, I suppose a hurricane is just one of many things that time includes. Another obvious fact is that resisting time is about as futile as resisting hurricane Hugo. Needless to say, one cannot change its course or turn it back. You just hold on and try to endure it.

In many ways time is the same. You cannot change its course or turn it back. You just hold on to and endure it. Fight it all you can, but it will beat you in the long run. Just as one has no choice but to submit to the hurricane, so must we submit to the force of time.

I admit that such a statement sounds terribly passive, even hostile. Such words certainly do not sound like the friendly status we want to grant time. The fact remains that time is something to which we must submit. A sense of resignation to time is not weakness but an indication of wisdom. Long ago Ralph Waldo Emerson pinned these words:

> Teach me your mood, O patient stars!
> Who climb each night the ancient sky
> Leaving on space no shade, no scars,
> No trace of age, no fear to die.

Please understand that I am not implying that all of these

things that we do to resist time are necessarily immoral. They are a little funny at times but not immoral. After all, there are a lot of industries whose existence depends on our fighting the effects of time. Where would the cosmetic industry be without the "fountain of youth" syndrome? There are those who color their hair. Others of us try to "plant a new garden" up there and usually end up with another bad crop. The fashion world feeds upon our desire to look young and be "with it." We have fat sucked out, new guide wires added for other parts, knees and elbows tucked, and faces lifted. Unfortunately, the only thing that really changes is our checking account.

If one can afford a contractor for all of these property improvements, fine. If it is a genuine attempt to add a little grace to the process of growing older, "have at it." But if you think that you are denying the march of time and that you are outsmarting it, you are in for a big let down. Time always wins—always.

To recognize the inevitability of time is not to take a pessimistic attitude toward life. Submitting to time only means we are wise enough to recognize the truth. Once we are on course with reality we can then position and prepare ourselves for the storm that is due. There are many things we can do to lessen the impact of a hurricane. We can build on better foundations, use better materials, recognize inherent currents, enjoy the sunny days while making the most of the cloudy ones, and not ignore the forecasters who say that a storm is coming. To ignore the call is a promise of loss. Well, I'm here to tell you that a storm is coming and its name is not Hugo.

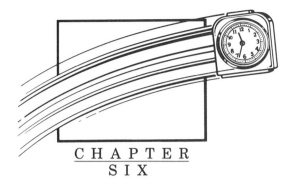

CHAPTER
SIX

Victim
of Circumstances

"Taking charge can . . ."

W henever possible I like to come home for lunch, but not for the reasons you might think. For one thing I'm cheap. Another reason is that the house is empty, and I can load up on peanut butter and vanilla wafers without listening to any words of warning or criticism. While I am enjoying two of the best things God ever created, I can turn on cable television and watch the reruns of Perry Mason. I like Perry because he always wins and the bad guy always confesses. The outcome of every story is one of the few things in life that is unquestionably predictable.

One day recently, I turned on the television; and before I got to Perry, I stopped on a movie channel which was showing an old, old movie. The scene was an ancient castle surrounded by a high wall and a deep moat. The people were being terrorized by a band of barbarians who surrounded them. The people within the castle seemed helpless, "planless," and hopeless. They were totally at the mercy of the barbarians and their own fears.

The castle which protected them seemed dark and cold. Very little light penetrated the thick walls which were to protect them from the outside enemy forces. Those who dwelled within could be best characterized by their spirit of fear. They appeared frozen in their protective environment, and their fears had turned those walls into a prison instead of a haven of safety. There was no plan, just passive resignation to their fears and the unidentifiable foe which resided outside somewhere.

As I sat and watched that old movie I began to see a reflection of the way many of us relate to time, especially the future. Since there is much we cannot change about time, a certain amount of resignation is necessary. We must accept the fact that life will bring changes. After all, a few wrinkles will add character to the brow. Hair will gray a bit or, as for some of us, fall out. One can celebrate his or her thirty-ninth birthday only so many times until even the slowest of the slow figure it out. Time brings inevitable changes.

But, does that mean we should seclude ourselves in a cold, dark castle and attempt to hide from the forces of time that surround us? Are we to take a passive stance toward time and assume a helpless, "planless," and hopeless position in the prison we build around us? A passive stance toward time is very unfortunate indeed.

Either we take a deliberative and operative attitude toward time or we become a victim. When we assume the victim's role, we find ourselves blaming our circumstances. Our constant refrain is, "We have no choice. We are victims of time."

Ask most people who are genuinely unhappy why they are so disconsolate, and they will tell you they are just "victims of circumstances." Their life has been forced upon them. In actuality the real problem is that they have taken very little responsibility for their lives and are satisfied to place the blame on time and circumstances. "What else could I do?"

I remember an experience many years ago when our daughter, Melody, was very young. She was having one of those bad days, when she seemed to be out of step with the whole world. She was in a horrible mood and was being generally hard to manage. After a reasonable amount of misbehavior Melody had reached the limits of her parents' patience. Suzanne and I held "court" and sentenced Melody to her room for the rest of the night. She was sent upstairs to her room, which only added to her frustration.

When the door of her room was closed, an uncharted hurricane suddenly moved through her room. There was crying, screaming, throwing, and making strange noises within those walls. We listened to make sure that she did not hurt herself but decided not to interrupt her. For one thing, we were curious as to how long this would go on.

Finally the hurricane passed and we decided to go in and inspect the damage. As I opened the door, I saw Melody sitting on the floor against the wall. She was totally exhausted and surrounded by a total disarray of toys and clothes. As I walked into her room, she looked at me with all the seriousness that a five year old could gather and said, "Look at what you made me do!" There is a point to the story.

Is that not generally the attitude we assume toward time? "Time does it to us!" We are helpless victims of the forces of time. We look at the disarray of our lives and say, "Time, look at what you made me do."

We must take responsibility and take charge of our time. Certainly we cannot control all things that come upon us any more than we can turn back the force of a hurricane. But we don't have to take a passive role in relationship to time. We do have some "say so" as to how we expend this allotment of time granted to us. An intentional approach makes a lot more sense.

The writer, Harold Kushner, makes an interesting point about the way we invest our time. "Ask the average person which is more important to him, making money or being devoted to his family, and virtually everyone will answer family without hesitation. But watch how the average person actually lives out his life."[1]

Why do we live such contradictory lives? The reason is that most of us have never fully taken responsibility for our lives. We are satisfied to place the blame on time and circumstances and say, "Look at what you made me do."

Life should be a deliberate act, not a passive response to circumstances. Otherwise we become subject to all the forces that surround us, and we find ourselves walled up in a dark and cold castle waiting for the next attack of the barbarians. One must make a conscious effort to take time seriously and be sensitive to how we spend this most valuable of resources.

What really is important to us? There is so often a difference between what we say is important and that to which we give ourselves. The most important investment we make in life has nothing to do with a bank or stock broker. It is the deliberate choice we make to take time seriously and take responsibility for the share that comes to us as a gift from the Father.

Quantity and Quality

Recently I was talking on the telephone with a friend. He was sharing some of his concerns about the fact that his schedule did not allow as much time as he would like to be with his children. I immediately came to his rescue because not only his guilt was the issue, but suddenly mine had been triggered.

I tried to ease his guilt by my standard lecture on, "It's not the quantity of time but rather the quality that counts with one's children." After all, I have soothed my own conscience on many occasions with this very simple answer.

Now I admit that there is some truth to the need for this "quality time." But, it can become a cop out. What happens when you apply this theory to some other areas of life?

You are traveling on a new section of interstate highway, and there is a long stretch of highway where no gas stations have yet been built. This is of great concern now that the car has come to a stop, because you are out of gas, and cars are hard to push! You hang out the help flag that you won at Burger Land eight years ago. A traveler stops, and you share your plight. He excuses himself for a moment. When he returns, he acknowledges his concern for your situation and indicates that he wants to help. He has taken from his own gas tank a medicine bottle full of gas.

You then remind him that the next gas station is many, many miles away and that a medicine bottle full of gas is not very much. He says, "But this is one of our nation's purest fuels and has a ninety-two octane rating. It is the best of quality!" Under the circumstances quantity does make a difference.

I remember an illustration in a sermon preached by Dr. John Claypool about the value of quality. It went something like this: "You've been looking forward all day to a good meal that night. You sit down at the table and your wife places before you a piece of steak which is one inch square. She reminds you that it is the finest piece of beef that can be bought." Quality is important and so is quantity.

Now back to the issue of time and children. Sometimes it is impossible to have long blocks of time. Therefore, one must make the best of what he can offer, but that does not do away with the fact that quantity is important. A part of the problem is that we use this "quality theory" as a way of justifying poor habits or simply relieving our guilt.

Relationships need time to grow. There is a need for time when people are free and open to talk, think, and even do nothing together. Most of the time we spend with our children is structured. The time is usually occupied with planned activity. If one's true thoughts and feelings are to be shared, time is a requirement. This is true for both parents and children. It is certainly needed between parent and child. Needless to say, it is a good investment in the relationship of a couple. With our children we need to remember that a quick ten minute game of checkers or computer game before bedtime one night a week does not necessarily fill the bill.

By all means, do not undercut the importance of those concentrated five minutes with Johnny or Sally. Those minutes are beyond value. But let's never allow those five minute sessions to be a "cop out" for quantity of time that family relationships need for growth and nourishment.

I told my good friend over the telephone that I was not totally honest. I must confess that my own guilt got in the way. I think we both knew the truth.

Priority of Family Time

I was attending a meeting on Sunday evening a few weeks ago. During some casual conversation I remember making the statement that, "I had been gone every night that week and that my family had not eaten an evening meal together all week long." Later on that night I kept rethinking the statement that I had made. It was bad enough that the statement was true, but it was even worse that it appeared that I was bragging about it. To have ignored the needs of one's family was certainly not anything to brag about. I should have been too ashamed to mention it.

The kind of world we live in does not enhance family life. There are demands that come from every direction, and many of these are extremely worthwhile. The pace, schedule, and responsibilities tend to pull a family apart rather than forcing them together.

A positive and healthy family life is a gift straight from God. It is one of the most refreshing and motivating forces in a person's life. But our pace is denying us of so much of its beauty. This routine panic is one of our worst enemies.

Family relationships have to be built and nourished and that takes time. Yet, for some reason we tend to think that everything else is more important. Our society is full of families who don't even know each other. They sleep in the same house, occasionally eat together, but seldom sit together and talk about the little personal things that are so important.

The real test of one's desire may come at this point. This may mean that one has to say no occasionally to outside demands or even back out of some existing responsibilities. There are few things in one's life more important than the family.

Children, today, more than ever are begging for their parent's time. Time to talk, walk, kick rocks, and do nothing together. The irony of it is that what our children are needing does not require money!

In retrospect I now can think back to so many nights when I would come in from work and Chris and Melody would meet me at the door and immediately ask, "How was work today, Daddy?" I am somewhat haunted now by the memory that so many times I would answer them very quickly and hurry on past them because there were only a few minutes to eat and be at another meeting. Frequently our priorities get out of order and need to be reviewed.

Nevertheless, if you have ever bragged about how many nights you have been away from home, think about it again. It should not be a source of pride. It should make us so guilty that we cannot stand it. Or better yet, do something about it while there is still the chance.

The Bible and Stewardship

We typically use the Bible as our primary text for the proper stewardship of money. The Bible is certainly not limited only to concerns about money. Why do we not emphasize the stewardship of time with the same intensity? Are we too passive?

Consider the powerful parable that our Lord told concerning the talents. The story is about a man who is traveling to a far country and calls in his servants. To one servant he gives five talents, to another he gives two, and to another one. The master takes his leave with a sense of trust in his servants. The man with five talents makes five more. The man with two gained two more. But the servant who received one very passively dug a hole and buried his "one" in order to protect it. He didn't abuse it, he just didn't do anything with it.

The master commended the man with five and the man with two, because they had been good stewards of what they had been given. The servant who hid his one was not only chastised but cast out of the kingdom. At first this may seem like a very audacious response to the man who really had not deliberately misused what he had been given. But then again, that was his problem. He had not done anything!

I have heard this text used for everything from the wise use of money to signing up new members for the choir. But one of the best applications of this parable is in regard to our time. We are not to passively dig a hole and bury it. We are not to be victims of our own fears and take no risks in the expenditure of the allotted time given us.

We are to take seriously the gifts of the Master and return to Him that which He has given us with interest. But we cannot do it, if we constantly assume the role of victim in regard to our time. Our use of time should be positive and intentional. Such an attitude is one of the marks of maturity and wisdom.

Growing Up

Taking responsibility for yourself means growing up. And growing up does not happen accidently. William James once said that the average person never achieves more than ten percent of the potential he has. If that is the truth we are all party to a tremendous waste of time and talent. Wasted time is wasted life. We certainly want to avoid the pain of the man in Jesus' parable of the talents who had to confess that he had done nothing with that which he had been given. The parable is very clear that Jesus looked with great disdain upon such foolish waste of time and circumstance.

If growth is measured by a sense of responsibility, how do we know that it is happening to us? Dr. John E. Johns, President of Furman University, wrote an article entitled "Come Grow With Us," in which he suggested a checklist of six indispensable marks of a mature person. They are worth passing on.

A grown-up person is one who has developed the capacity to be interested in and concerned about other people rather than himself. The newborn infant is a bundle of self-centered needs capable of almost limitless expansion of his horizon to include the world. But at first he is only concerned for his hunger, his discomfort, his pain, or his security. The process of becoming a grown-up is that beautiful drama of reaching out to others, shifting the focus from oneself to others.

The grown-up person has learned the place of self-discipline in life. One of the marks of the child is that he has to have somebody to discipline him. The mature person does what he needs to do, whether he likes it or not. Winifred Rhoades, a psychologist, said, "If you're not a grown up, you escape what you don't want to do. You try to get results in easier ways." The mature person does what needs to be done when it isn't fun.

The mature person has the capacity to absorb the shock of

disappointment, the frustration of defeat, the blow of afflic-
tion, and the terrible burden of grief. A mature mind is not
locked in the closed position. It can change. We simply do not
go sailing through life with never a rough sea or bad voyage.

The grown-up takes responsibility. He does not insist, like
a child, that life always be fun and games. I am talking about
the kind of person who cops out whenever responsibility is
called for, the kind of person who never gets his mind in gear
with his God-given talents to do anything worthwhile.

The mature person is able to deny himself an immediate
gain in order to have a long-range value. We are encouraged
in this immature behavior by television which offers 'instant
satisfaction' of every human want.

The grown-up person has come to terms with the ultimate
meaning of life. In short, he has not avoided the ultimate
questions: What does life mean? What is its source? What is
its purpose and destination? How do I get in touch with the
ultimate reality of God?[2]

Spending Wisely

Most of us discovered long ago that a given amount of
money can only be spent once. In spite of our wish to the
contrary a dollar bill can only be spent one time. We may
have tried to spend it twice, but we found out quickly that it
can only be used once.

This particular fact forces us to make decisions. If we
have one dollar in our pocket, we must decide how it will be
used. And when it is gone, it is gone! Hopefully, we used it
wisely. We forget, however, that our time has that same
characteristic. From somewhere we have developed the attitude that time is unlimited; and therefore, our usage of it is
not a very big issue. After all, there is plenty where the last
came from.

Unfortunately, time is a commodity like money in that it
can only be used once. A given moment of time can be spent

only once. When it is gone, it is gone. And that moment of time deserves the same respect and careful stewardship as does the dollar bill.

This fact also forces us to make decisions. And some of these decisions take on ethical dimensions. Just as we can choose to spend all of the dollar bill on ourselves, we can do the same with our time. We have that option and certainly the temptation is to do so.

We can choose to use some of that time for concerns other than our own. And this means that when it is gone, it is still gone. We can't always spend it on someone else and ourselves. The decision sometimes becomes a matter of either us or them.

Time is a valuable gift from God. Like our money it can only be spent once. There are times in our lives (daily, in fact) when we must decide on whom a given moment of time will be spent.

Notes

1. Harold Kushner, *When All You've Ever Wanted Isn't Enough* (New York: Summit Books, 1986), 15.
2. John E. Johns, "Come Grow With Us," *The New Age Magazine* (Washington, D. C.: The Supreme Council, 1989), 116:9, 21.

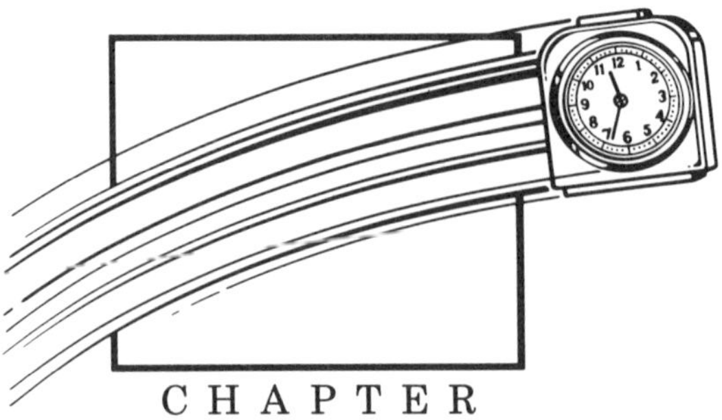

CHAPTER
SEVEN

Dealing with Change

"You will have tribulation; but be of good cheer. . ."
(John 16:33).

We all have occasionally heard back-porch philosophers say that, "The only two things in life that one can count on are death and taxes." There is definitely a hint of truth in such a statement, but it is obviously incomplete. There are other things in life that one can count on, and the one that most quickly comes to my mind is change. Few things are more predictably a part of our existence than that of change.

Struggling against change is like fighting against gravity. You can deny and ignore it all you want to but defy it and it will break your bones. Our approval or disapproval has no bearing on the reality of change that occurs continuously around us.

Since change is inseparably related to the issue of time, we must, therefore, develop some kind of "livable" philosophy of change, if time is to ever take on the status of friend. We can spend our days and nights denying and even fighting change, but change goes right along whether we acknowledge it or not.

Another dimension which we must consider is the theological implications of one's attitude toward change. Our attitude toward change is very much a religious issue. For example, is God a static God? Is His work a finished reality? Did He do "it" back then and that was the end of it? Or is God always in the process of bringing into being? One's attitude toward change is an intensely theological issue and may say more about our understanding of God than we would like to admit.

Michael J. Brooks, writing for the Baptist Bulletin Service, has said,

> Many people refuse to consider change at all. They reason that if something has been acceptable for so long, why modify or reject it? The problem here is the old way may not be the best way. Jesus came preaching a new covenant, but the Jewish leaders chose rather to hold to their traditions and to reject Him. What a tragedy! The closed mind is like a stagnated pond.

In the Beginning

If we are to rethink our perception of change, we must go back, all the way to the history of creation. What is our understanding of the creation story? What did God really do "in the beginning"? Was perfection the result of God's creation experience? According to Scripture He looked at what had been created and said, "It was very good!" (Gen. 1:31). But, was it perfection in the sense that nothing else ever needed to be done?

When I think of a perfect painting, I assume that not one more stroke could ever be added. It is a finished product and needs nothing from anyone ever again. When I perceive something as perfect, I am making an assumption that it is a complete product. Is that the way Genesis describes the creation story? "It was good," but was it a finished product?

On the first day God created light and separated it from the darkness. "God saw the light, that it was good; and God divided the light from the darkness" (v. 4).

The second day of creation brought into being the firmament. "Then God said, 'Let there be a firmament in the midst of the waters, and let it divide the waters from the waters'" (v. 6). God called this firmament heaven.

On the third day God created the dry land and brought forth the grass and all the herb bearing seed. Fruit came about and the earth began to produce. The Genesis writer then constructs a beautiful image when he says, "God saw that it was good" (v. 12).

The fourth day witnessed the creation of the lights of the firmament. The sun and the moon would divide the days from the nights. He said also of this part, "It is good" (v. 18).

On the fifth day God brought into being the sea creatures and every winged bird; and once again, God said, "It was good" (v. 21). And then He blessed them by saying, "'Be fruitful and multiply, and fill the waters in the seas, and let birds multiply on the earth'" (v. 22).

The sixth day witnessed an interesting phenomenon. Not only did He create the beast of the earth but moved on to the climax of His creation. "Let Us make man in Our image, according to Our likeness" (v. 26). At that point we read one of the most affirming statements in all of Holy Scripture. "God saw everything that He had made, and indeed it was very good" (v. 31). What a beautiful affirmation of creation and especially of man!

On the seventh day we are told that God rested, which is something that many of us have long forgotten. He rested from His labors. The *New King James Version* describes the scene as, "He rested from all His work which God had created and made" (2:3). I am not a Hebrew scholar, and my seminary professors would affirm that fact, but I dare say that the construction of that verb would mean that He rested from all the work He had done thus far.

We do not read that on the seventh day He quit and retired, never to create again. The Bible says very simply, "He rested." I do not believe that He ceased to be involved in the creating business. He just rested.

How much better can one describe the creation account than a story of change? It was phenomenal change that could only have been orchestrated by the Lord of Creation. But, it was not the end of creation, and therefore, it was not the end of change. Change is one of the ways God works.

The creative work of God continues on to this very minute. He is constantly bringing life into being, bringing form out of the void. I visited a young mother in the hospital. She had a new baby. She named him David Charles, and he is one of God's special creations. He is not something reincarnated from that first creation. He is brand new. God is still hovering over the face of the waters and bringing life out of the formless deep (see Gen. 1:2).

This morning I got up early and quickly became busy at my familiar keyboard. I could hardly think and type because of my preoccupation with the rising sun. The colors were absolutely beautiful. There have been many sunrises, but every one of them is unique. The colors of this morning's sunrise will never be reproduced. There has never been one like this one, just like there will never be one like the design of tomorrow morning. I am reminded by the stage of this morning's drama that God is still creating.

As I watch my children grow, I am reminded that God is still creating. They are constantly changing. They leave behind some things and pick up some new things. They begin to put away some childish ways and take on new ways. Change is the bottom line.

This evening, like most other Tuesday and Thursday evenings, I picked up Melody from her ballet class. I enjoy arriving a few minutes early so that I can observe her working out. She and her fellow students work very hard. Ballet is a strenuous discipline. As a result, new muscles will emerge. Her strength will increase, and poise and grace will develop. God continues to create.

On Valentine's Day one year Melody received an unsolicited greeting card in the mail from her brother Chris who is away at college. This brother who until recently would go to great lengths to keep from being seen in public with his sister and now sends her a Valentine greeting. Unquestionably, God is still creating!

The point I am making is that God did not cease with His creative activity with the conclusion of the Genesis account. I believe He rested, just like the Bible says. But I believe God is creating right now, at this very moment. Change is the bottom line. Change is not foreign to God. While not all change is from God, we need to be careful not to write off all change as evil. It can be envisioned as His instrument.

Creation Upward or Downward?

In which direction is creation moving? Are we on a downward spiral toward disintegration or are we in a collaborative venture with the Creator? Are we on a frightening course of self-destruction, or are we moving toward some kind of great climax in history? The answer we give has a great deal of bearing on our attitude toward change. According to the Genesis account humans drastically changed God's original plan for His "experiment" on this earth.

Within the freedom granted by God, humans turned over the vast table prepared for them by God. Because of what we did in the garden, we became our own worst enemy and forever influenced the relationship humans were to enjoy with the Creator.

Fortunately for us, God was not willing to give up on this experiment and made another attempt to bring humankind back into partnership with Him. "In the fullness of time" God entered history and once again restated His plan to share life with those created in His image. While many refused to hear what He said, a Way was still provided.

A part of the statement made by God was that there would come a day when the earth as we know it would end. "With the voice of the archangel, and with the trumpet of God" (1 Thess. 4:16), the Lord would return, and time as we now experience it would be no more.

Does this mean that God is now tired of this costly experiment and ready to call it all off? I realize that there will be judgment, but the end of time will not occur because God is frustrated with humankind. The end of time will not come about because human beings have been so evil, and there will eventually be a "final straw" so that God says, "Enough, I've had enough!" Then He wipes history away, and the form becomes void again.

Unquestionably, there will be a second coming of our Lord, and there will be an "end time." Indeed there will be judgment, but the second coming should never be envisioned as the final straw. It will just be the end of this stage of His plan. An exciting transition will occur for all who have believed in His Name. Time will become timeless. All things will become new. In ways that we cannot imagine on this side of that experience, everything will be different.

I envision the end of time as another positive move by a God who is always creating, giving, and sharing Himself. The key word for me is *positive* rather than negative. I do not perceive God as a distant power who finds satisfaction in observing His creation's self-destruction.

I do not question that humans "fouled up" big time in the garden and drastically changed God's plan. But, I do not perceive history as a downward spiral toward destruction as a result of humankind's sins. We cannot escape the consequences of original sin. However, God is a creative God and continues to invite us to work with Him in a world that He created, because He wanted to share life.

The world may self-destruct. However, it will not be because God wants it that way. His desire is to work as a partner with us and collaborate with us. He is not a sadistic parent who takes pleasure as He watches His children "do themselves in."

If we would only move close to the One in whose image we are created and collaborate with Him, the changes in life that we dread and condemn could become a positive and exciting venture. The problem is not with a God who likes to keep us guessing and insecure. The problem is with humans who have never really learned to use the freedom that is a part of God's created order.

Not all change is of God. Some of it is a consequence of our sin. Yet, let us take heed not to assume that all change is of Satan. Change is one way that God is constantly drawing humans, the climax of His creation, closer to Him.

The Role of Struggle

Change also comes as a result of our own struggle. We have done ourselves an injustice by also perceiving struggle as evil. I agree that some of our struggle comes as a result of our own ineptness. But, not all struggle is of Satan.

John's Gospel records an interesting conversation of Jesus with His disciples. He was trying to give them a glimpse of what the future held for them. He was telling them about His own rejection and the extreme pain and sorrow that would overshadow their lives. He certainly was not painting a picture of a worry-free life.

Then Jesus made a statement that at first glance might seem paradoxical. He said, " 'These things I have spoken to you, that in Me you may have peace. In the world you will have tribulation; but be of good cheer, I have overcome the world' " (John 16:33). Two very unusual statements linked together in the same thought—peace and tribulation. What a strange combination!

Jesus was not talking in the abstract but rather from His own personal experience. He was not predicting anything for our lives that was not a part of His own. He did not promise to rescue us from struggle but promised to be our companion in life. He said, " 'I have overcome the world.' " And through Him we do the same. But struggle and tribulation are still a part of the expected order. Struggle must evidently be one of the ways that God guides us along the path. And struggle inherently implies change. When we open ourselves to the possibility of struggle and change, we free ourselves to a whole new future. It is much more than just taking off blinders. It is more like cutting the rope that holds us to limited possibilities.

Dr. John Claypool has stated it well,

> When we stop expecting rescue and open up to resource, not only does Jesus Christ come alive as our Companion; the whole Bible also takes on new life! No longer is it an abstract book about far-off people; it now becomes "the communion of the saints," "a cloud of witnesses"—the story of people who, like ourselves, had to struggle, and who can teach us something from their lives that can strengthen us for our own coping.[1]

My point is that the Christian life does not protect us from struggle, and it certainly does not insulate us from change. Instead, we are given strength to cope and even do something better than that. We are enabled to envision God within our lives, when the critical path is not a straight line but rather a broken line from one struggle to another. That is not pessimism but a deep breath of freedom for one who has perceived change as a threat as well as an instrument of evil.

I totally agree with the statement, "Jesus Christ is the same yesterday, today, and forever" (Heb. 13:8). He is constant amidst a changing world. He remains static, while we do not. He is not on a journey, but we are. Even the great moment that the Christian awaits is described as change: "Behold, I tell you a mystery: We shall not all sleep, but we shall all be changed" (1 Cor. 15:51). And that big change in life is preceded by thousands of little ones that lead all the way to that moment.

In the sixteenth century St. Francis De Sales wrote:

> Do not look forward to the changes and chances of this life in fear; rather look to them with full hope that, as they arise, God, whose you are will deliver you out of them. He has kept you hitherto, do you but hold fast to His dear Hand, and He will lead you safely through all things; and, when you cannot stand, He will bear you in His arms. Do not look forward to what may happen tomorrow; the same everlasting Father who cares for you today, will take care of you tomorrow, and every day. Either He will shield you from suffering, or He will give you unfailing strength to bear it. Be at peace then, and put aside all anxious thoughts and imaginations.

Some Things Unchanged

Not everything in life is fluid. There is a great deal in life that is constant. Otherwise, there would be no sense of stability. I could name many, but for the moment allow me to mention just one personal anchor in a sea of change. Consider the anchor of memory. Memory is a constant, and it frequently reminds us of other things that are as well. Our memories are very special gifts from God. I make such a statement after a very brief trip to my hometown to visit my aunt. My son was home from college, and the two of us made a very rushed trip to LaGrange, Georgia. I seldom see my aunt, and this seemed like a good way to spend a day.

Being in her house is always a pleasant experience. It is the same house that my grandmother and grandfather lived in, when I was growing up. To be in that house for even a few minutes allows me to transcend time for a brief moment. I don't get back to the area of my roots very often, and when I do, I am affected by the experience.

I cannot help but remember so many of the good experiences that took place in that house, particularly at times such as Christmas and other special seasons of the year. There was a lot of love in that house, and I felt a genuine sense of belonging. There was never any need to be accepted. That was a given. I was a grandchild, and that was all the entrance requirement needed.

The woods on one side of the house were full of adventure. They seemed so big then. We fought the "yankees" in those woods; we defeated enemies on many occasions! Now the woods are the home of a commercial greenhouse. The few woods that are left are quiet, and they don't seem so big any more.

The creek that ran behind the house always had a fish or two in it. And it seemed like the Atlantic ocean then. I am sure that it is the same size now that it was then, but it doesn't seem like it would provide much of a fishing trip now. It surely did then.

The pasture is all grown up and so thick you can hardly walk through it now. It was open and green then, which was a good thing for my Dad on the day that he roped a cow and in the excitement forgot to let go of the other end of the rope. The cow dragged him through the grass and through the creek before he remembered to let go.

I can still identify with the sense of freedom that I felt in my grandparents' house. They always had time for whatever you wanted to do. Their love was unconditional. Like

God's love, it was just there, no strings. There was no interest or pay back.

A lot of things have changed since then. So much time has passed since I roamed those woods, spent a Friday night, raided the apple tree, or waited on the porch for my Granddad to come home from the shoe shop. But even now, many years later, I still feel the love there. It is in the smells, trees, and walls. Time has not changed that.

In the midst of change there is the unchanged. The love we experience from special people remains constant. It is one of those things that does not change nor does it occur in isolation. God touches our faces through such people. Through them we are reminded that God's love is always a constant. Change is a part of life, but thanks be to God for His love which never varies. Some things in life do not change.

Note

1. John Claypool, *The Light Within You* (Waco: Word Incorporated, 1983), 126.

CHAPTER
EIGHT

Use of Time

"Rocking and singing . . ."

One of the real tragedies of our culture is the loss of oral tradition. By oral tradition I simply mean the practice of story telling—the passing down of stories relating to religion, family, and personal history. Especially important is the passing along of family history. Who has time to tell stories any more? We are seldom in one place long enough. If we are, the television is the center of attention, and conversation can take place only during the commercials.

Story telling takes time. Who has time for such trivia, or so it seems to most people. And why should we tell anything when there are video camera recorder's and computers which have taken the place of our memory? The computer in my study at home can keep track of my schedule for the next fifty years and prompt me of important events. It can maintain my checkbook and balance it with the bank. Notice that I said that it "can." I tried it, and it blew every fuse in the house. It kept flashing some kind of high-tech computer language saying, "insufficient funds." My manual had nothing about it so I chose to ignore the command.

Anyway, I thoroughly enjoy hearing the stories of my family. Occasionally my parents will talk about their parents, grandparents, and the experiences of family members long forgotten, which in itself is very unfortunate. My mother was recently remembering some of her childhood experiences; and, quite naturally, many of those stories surround my grandmother. She was a very special woman.

Especially when I think of using time wisely, my thoughts frequently go back to my grandmother. My remembrance comes from my own experience and the stories that my mother has passed on to me. There are so many good memories that I have of her. One in particular is how comfortable she seemed to be with the passing of time. In recent days my appreciation of that quality in her life has grown.

There seemed to be so little struggle in her life with things that bother me. She was usually busy but seldom rushed. There was a sense of acceptance that characterized her days. Her life was filled with changes like everyone else. Yet, the changes that time brought were, by appearance, willingly received by her. That was just one reason she was such a pleasant person to be with.

My mother and I were recently discussing how well my grandmother used time. There always seemed to be time to do the important things, and to this day I cannot ever recall my grandmother rushing around in a way that so characterizes my life.

When my mother was a young girl, my grandparents moved to the mill village in LaGrange, Georgia. My mother's brother and sister were older and were already working outside the home. My mother, even now, tells that one of her very warm memories is that of coming home from school every day; and as she approached her house, my grandmother would be rocking on the porch and singing. Such a simple frame of memory but a potent one for me.

What makes that rocking and singing special is the kind of demands upon my grandmother's life. She cooked three meals each day for everyone in the house. Since three members worked outside the home on three different shifts, that meant she must prepare dinner and supper three different times. The meals were always "full meals" and hot.

The clothes were washed by hand, always starched, and perfectly ironed. Her house was always immaculate, the yard raked with a cane broom, and practically all the clothes made with a foot pumped sewing machine. With all of that going on, she found time to rock and sing on the front porch, usually when my mother came home from school. That image absolutely overwhelms my imagination. When was the last time you saw anyone rocking and singing on the front porch with everything else in their life in order?

I realize that many of us have memories of grandmothers who had time for us. There were few things in their lives that were as important as the current needs of a grandchild. But my preoccupation with my grandmother's life-style goes beyond the stereotyped image. There was a beautiful sense of ease about her life that I seldom enjoy.

Possibly that sense of acceptance came from her rural background. In the country there was an apparent sensitivity to the seasons. There was a cyclical rhythm to life that most of us have lost. Now we have little or no sensitivity to the seasons. Our homes are maintained at a constant temperature by computerized thermostats.

About the only time we notice the difference between summer and winter is when we make the journey from our house to our automobile which is also thermostatically controlled. Seasons mean very little to us except for a slight change in fashions, which are purchased at the mall, in which one would never know the difference between night and day.

There were certain rituals that added meaning to the seasons. In the spring you planted a garden, which was harvested and canned in the summer, to be enjoyed in the fall and winter. Today if you were to ask my children where string beans come from, they would immediately say the grocery store.

Plants were brought in for the winter and put back out in the spring. Firewood was cut in the spring, dried out in the summer, and burned in the winter. There were some very normal routines that tied the seasons together, yet each one had a special purpose.

As my generation moved to the suburbs, we also moved away from a certain rhythm that added meaning to life. It was a rhythm that affirmed a natural flow to life. Why would one want to fight something that seems so natural and predictable? Birth, growth, and death were just the way they were meant to be. You didn't fight them; you moved with them, affirmed them, and celebrated them. Now we seem to mourn this natural rhythm.

In our habits and obsessions we try to deny the influences of time, which really does not make a lot of sense. How can we ignore the inevitable? To do so is like ignoring the law of gravity. To do so is to break one's bones.

Permit me to refer once again to my grandmother. From my own personal knowledge I would like to suggest three commendable qualities of her life that linger in my memory, that also might be worth passing along to you. I cannot honestly say that I have incorporated them into my own life, but I am trying.

Acceptance

First, there was a very positive acceptance of life's passages. I still think some of that came from her rural background. The ground was prepared. The seed was planted. The field was worked. The crop was harvested. The field was turned and awaited the cycle to begin again.

Do not misunderstand me. I did not grow up in ancient Phoenecia, and I do not believe that history moves only in a cycle. I identify with the biblical understanding of time as moving in a line, going somewhere. History is the story of God's revelation of Himself to humankind. Time has purpose, a destination.

Yet, my image of time is enhanced by envisioning it as a forward moving spiral rather than a straight line. It is not an aimless circle with no plan or purpose. It is a forward process with a natural rhythm that adds meaning and predictability to its movement.

To celebrate the rhythm of life is to add depth and beauty to the inevitable passing of time. Our culture is guilty of denying that cyclical rhythm. We have developed the false image that life is supposed to be constant. We seek to insulate ourselves from the cyclical nature of life by some expensive methods. We purchase insurance on everything from our possessions to our very breath. This will supposedly protect us from the inevitable crises. Our computerized thermostats keep our surroundings at a constant temperature year round. Our savings accounts and annuities will secure our financial resources against the short falls.

I am not against creature comforts. Even a casual observation of my life-style will affirm that. The point I am making is that life is not a constant line on the graph. There are ups and downs that we cannot ignore. But, more importantly, there is a rhythm to life that is not an accident. It is a part of God's plan.

The writer of Ecclesiastes discovered this:
> To everything there is a season,
> A time for every purpose under heaven:
> A time to be born,
> And a time to die;
> A time to plant,
> And a time to pluck what is planted;
> A time to kill,
> And a time to heal;
> A time to break down,
> And a time to build up;
> A time to weep,
> And a time to laugh;
> A time to mourn,
> And a time to dance (Eccl. 3:1-4).

Oliver Wendell Holmes once penned the words:

Build thee more stately mansions, O my soul,
As the swift seasons roll!
Leave thy low-vaulted past!
Let each new temple, nobler than the last,
Shut thee from heaven with a dome more vast,
Till thou at length art free,
Leaving thine outgrown shell by life's unresting sea.

In the words of Jesus: " 'For the earth yields crops by itself: first the blade, then the head, after that the full grain in the head' " (Mark 4:28).

Distractions

A second quality of my grandmother's life, that I would commend, was the absence of so many distractions. Have you ever taken notice of all that screams for your attention in the course of one day? Some of these distractions are from the very things that are supposed to make life easy for us. In our home there is something "on the blink" all the time. If it isn't the refrigerator, it is the television. The can opener broke this morning. The hot tub on the porch has a leak somewhere inside. The furnace is on its last leg. All four vehicles in my back yard need to have the oil changed.

If the creature comforts aren't demanding our attention, look at the schedule we keep. We want our children to have all the opportunities available to humankind, and many are very worthwhile. So we run from one "life sustaining" event to another. An extra long red light at one intersection will throw the whole day out of sync. I am not suggesting that these activities are not wholesome and virtuous. But, where are the quiet moments with no pushing and rushing, time to think aloud together. Could it be, however, that instead of shoving our children from one social event to another, from ballet to piano to tap to violin to soccer, we might do well to occasionally sit on the porch and tell them about one of their strange relatives who used to collect flies for a hobby?

Many of us would do well by to examine what is really important in our lives. Establishing a sense of priorities in our lives does not mean that lesser things are dishonorable. It means that we cannot do everything. It means that we cannot be in two places at one time. We cannot be in one place comfortably, if we are anxious about the fact that we are supposed to be somewhere else in ten minutes, and we are ten miles away. Distractions are a real problem for many of us.

Quiet, But Strong Faith

A third quality of my grandmother that I cannot ignore was her quiet sense that there was not only rhyme to her life but reason as well. Her strong faith showed there was no question that God was involved in her life. Life was no accident. He had placed her in that time and in that setting and with a particular man, and she was very comfortable with God's range of choices for her life. She sought to make her surroundings better, but she didn't have to reject it to do so. There was no anger about her time, place, and circumstance. She did not spend her day trying to be someone else, at some other place, in some other time.

She would tell you confidently that God loved her and walked with her daily. Her life belonged to Him; and every aspect of her life was influenced by that faith, including her use and understanding of time. There was more in her life than that which could be seen by the eyes and touched with the fingers. There was something very comforting that undergirded and overarched her days. Too many of us have never experienced that sense of confidence.

I continue to go back in my mind to the image of my grandmother rocking and singing on the front porch, everything in relatively good order, and waiting on my mother to come home from school. To be honest, I cannot recall ever sitting, rocking, singing, and waiting on my children to come in from anywhere.

Booker T. Washington once described a fallacy of our educational system in that we no longer study the lives of great persons. One of those great persons for me was my grandmother, and I didn't realize it until it was too late to thank her.

Being Present to Time

"Always somewhere else . . ."

In the next few pages I want to introduce you to a thief. Chances are you have met this robber before. This culprit is guilty of stealing from us in quiet and subtle ways. The loss we experience cannot be replaced, is not covered by any insurance company, and is as precious as life itself. In fact, it is life. It is our time. Permit me to introduce this thief to you in a round about way, by means of a personal experience.

Living in the Present

Many preachers are familiar with a particular institution called a pulpit committee or pastoral search committee. You know you are really "in high cotton," when you are visited by a pastor selection committee. Regardless of their title, their job is the same throughout the land. Their purpose is to visit other churches and eventually "steal" a preacher. The fascinating thing is that it is all legal and expected. In many cases it is even encouraged.

For example, there are some cases when the presence of a committee can be a welcomed sight for both preacher and church. For the preacher, it can mean being found by the church for which you were eternally destined and have just

81

been "on hold" waiting to be discovered. If you are a member of a church that is having "health" problems (in other words, they are sick of their preacher) this may be the committee that will claim, call, and carry him far away. So, in the process of a committee's thievery some good things can occasionally occur.

My purpose at this point, however, is not to discuss the pros and cons of the pulpit committee phenomenon, which might be fun to do. I mention it only to provide a little background for the next few paragraphs.

For the past several months I have been dealing with a search committee from a church in another town. I say search committee, because this was a certified downtown church! They came as result of a recommendation by a friend. Our conversations were the routine kinds of discussions that take place between visiting committees and nervous preachers.

In fact, our conversations took place over a period of several months. We spent many hours discussing various subjects common to churches and ministers. After a rather long period of time, the process began to break down, as it occasionally does when it is not the Lord's will.

However, during this rather lengthy period of time a particular dynamic began to take place in my life. (Preachers can easily relate to what I am about to say.) In spite of the promise you make to yourself that you are not going to emotionally remove yourself prematurely from the present circumstances, inevitably some of this takes place. If the prospective situation seems inviting, it is almost impossible not to emotionally separate yourself and begin to live in the future.

One begins to live as if he or she had already moved. In some cases the prospect of the move is far from a definite thing. But, in your mind you begin to live "out there" in the future, as if there is no other frame of time. In spite of your best efforts the obsession is to live "out there" somewhere.

This is precisely where I found myself. Almost every aspect of my life became prefaced with "what if." In almost every dimension of my daily routine, I began to think in terms of a potential move. Daily decisions became colored by the remote chance that a move was ensuing. The end result has been that there were several months which have almost been erased from my recollection. The reason is obvious. I have been living ahead of myself. I have been so tied up with the future that, as a result, I have given little attention to the present time.

I have talked with others who have gone through the same kind of experience. They have been guilty of doing the same thing. You have a brief experience with a committee and suddenly you jump into the future with both feet. One can become almost obsessed with "what if."

This is not a dilemma reserved only for preachers. Anyone is subject to the temptation. A potential new job looms bright on the horizon. Maybe this is the big step you have awaited for so long. Suddenly the present becomes a blur. The future becomes the only frame of reference.

We are all tempted at times to do this, not just in relationship to a new job but for events as well. One of the biggest temptations in life is that of living "out there" somewhere, running ahead of ourselves. When this becomes our characteristic way of relating, we sacrifice a great segment of our time, the present tense, which is by far the most usable of all dimensions of time.

Knowing the Importance of the Present

One of the most insightful descriptions of this problem was in a sermon preached by Dr. John Claypool. Much of my own sensitivity to this issue comes from the seed planted by that sermon. The sermon was entitled "Living in the Now" and was an honest confession of his own struggle to avoid living in times other than the present.

The scriptural text for the sermon was taken from the Mark 5 which is an intriguing description of one particular day in the life of Jesus. In the text, for example, Jesus has just arrived on the other side of the Sea of Galilee following His rebuking of the storm. He was immediately confronted by a demon-possessed man. In the exchange that followed Jesus healed the man of the evil spirits which then entered a herd of swine. The result of this action brought the scorn of the owners on Jesus.

In what would appear to be a fruitless search for some solitude, Jesus then crossed the lake again only to be confronted by another desperate man, named Jairus. This man, however, had a sick daughter. He pleaded with Jesus to heal this daughter who was at the point of death. Jesus honored his request and followed.

A significant event occurred on the way to Jairus' house as Jesus became aware that He had been touched by someone. It was by a woman who had been sick with a hemorrhage for twelve years. Now, the surprising dynamic in this story is not the fact that this woman was healed. Why should the healing of someone by Jesus be considered anything but normal?

As Dr. Claypool points out in his sermon, the fascinating feature of this story is that, with all that is "pulling" at Jesus, He maintained the presence and clarity of mind to know that someone had touched Him. People were pressing Him from all sides. With all the demands of the present moment, He was sensitive to the fact that someone had touched Him. It is intriguing that with all the possible apprehension Jesus was so in touch with the present moment.

During this walk to the home of Jairus, Jesus could have been oriented to the future. Many questions could have been offered. Will He arrive in time to make some changes, before everything and everybody become too involved? Will the daughter be alive or dead? What will be the emotional state of the family? These would be legitimate concerns of anyone in those circumstances. He had every right to be concerned about the future.

Jesus could also have been caught up in the events of the past few hours. Surely He was aware of His need for rest. And yet He was continually being interrupted. How frustrating that must have been! The temptation would have been extremely great to become caught up in the past. A little self-pity could easily be justified. After all, everyone deserves a little time and space. Everyone has limits.

Instead, Jesus was so cognizant of present circumstances that He was mindful of a sick woman who touched Him. She did not push Him. She did not make a scene. She did not call attention to herself. She just touched Him—a mere touch. In so doing, He demonstrated an awareness of the present that is phenomenal; an awareness we all should envy. Most of us, however, are so caught up in the past or future that we are almost oblivious to the present, and that is sad. Look at what we miss.

I recently counseled with a woman who was distressed. She had recently gone through a divorce. Then came the first Christmas after the divorce. It was a difficult time. She was astute and had already put her finger on part of her problem. Throughout Christmas she constantly seesawed between two preoccupations.

First, Christmas made her "think back." She constantly recalled the days when everyone was together, when the family was in tact. She became despondent as she remembered how it used to be. It is quite natural for us to reflect during this time of year, but her memory became a haunting force, an unrelenting one.

Second, there were also thoughts about what the future

would bring. How would she ever manage to financially support the needs of a daughter and son? Where would they be living when the next Christians rolled around? Would there be someone else someday to share Christmas, when the children were grown and gone? The future held many unanswered questions.

However, the immediate frustration for her was that she had become so caught up in "remembering when" and worrying about "what if" that Christmas came and went with little observation of the faces of her children. She had become almost oblivious to the joy that she assumed her children had experienced. Her past and future had covered her perception of the present moment. She was sad. She had missed some precious moments that could never be recovered. Are we not all guilty of the same behavior?

Dr. Gary Bagley of Meridian, Mississippi, has recently written in his weekly church newsletter: "To those who try to live in the future, tomorrow never comes. To those who try to live in the past, today is never an option. But to those who live life to the fullest as it occurs, God gives His blessings with the ability to dream dreams and see visions and recall the beauty of a blessed event."

The temptation is so great to become caught up in times that really do not belong to us. The older I become, the more I appreciate the way Jesus "did life." From what I read about Him in the New Testament, He seemed to do life so differently. He seemed to be so in control, aware, and in touch with Himself.

He accomplished much during His days on earth. The Gospel narratives paint a picture of Him never being out of breath nor out of sorts with Himself or His circumstances. I cannot help but ask, "How did He do it? What did He do differently?" And while the reasons may be many, one certainly must be His phenomenal ability to be "present to the present," sensitive to the current moment. He undoubtedly had a clear vision of the future, to eternal things. Yet, He was clearly anchored to the present.

Teaching to Live in the Present

The lessons He taught were examples of His sensitivity to the current moment. His teachings were filled with illustrations taken from things within immediate view. To do so required a tremendous sensitivity to the current moment.

For example, in the most powerful sermon ever preached, Jesus taught a practical lesson on the waste of worry. As He taught, He utilized objects that were in view of His followers. With phenomenal sensitivity He called attention to the birds which were within sight. He said, " 'Look at the birds of the air, for they neither sow nor reap nor gather into barns; yet your heavenly Father feeds them. Are you not of more value than they?' " (Matt. 6:26).

He went on to point to the lilies. He said, " 'Consider the lilies of the field, how they grow: they neither toil nor spin' " v. 28).

My point is that He had an amazing awareness of the present moment to be able to call attention to such appropriate illustrations. In His lesson about worry He gave the secret of His ability. In verse 34 He concluded, " 'Therefore do not worry about tomorrow, for tomorrow will worry about its own things. Sufficient for the day is its own trouble.' "

His parables were filled with illustrations that were right before the eyes of His listeners. They did not have to go to the local library to grasp His point. All they had to do was look around. And, I might add, at things to which most of us are oblivious.

Being Sensitive to the Present

The reason most of us are so insensitive to the present moment is that usually we are somewhere else. Either we are preoccupied with something that has already happened, something we cannot change. Or we are overwhelmed with the prospect of some potential event in the future, something that probably will not occur anyway. The bottom line is we have allowed ourselves to be robbed of present joys.

There is no greater thief of our time than the temptation to be somewhere else other than where we are, either preoccupied with the past or caught up in the future. The result is that we have been robbed.

As a parent I can think of many times when my children have approached me with something important to them. As was frequently the case, the moment they approached was really not a good time. I was busy with something that seemed important at the moment and quietly resented the interruption. So I brushed them away either by my response or the lack of one.

I remember distinctly an experience that occurred many years ago when my son, who is now grown, was just a toddler. One day I came home for lunch, which was my normal routine. Chris was in that stage of life when just being around his dad was something that excited him, a stage that is too brief. Most of that brevity can be attributed to dads who are too busy. On that particular day, the morning had not gone well. There were problems that had to be solved that day.

The whole time I was at home my mind was somewhere else. I ate my lunch with the family and was anxious to go back to my office. In my preoccupation I walked out the front door and started to get into my car. I heard a window in the living room open, and it was Chris who said, "That's OK Daddy, you can kiss me good-bye when you come in tonight."

During those few minutes at home, I had not solved a single problem that had to be faced that day, but I had certainly missed out on some special moments that could never be repeated. The reason was simple. I was so caught up in a combination of past problems and future solutions that the present ceased to exist.

Just think of what we miss. Many of life's most precious moments are not planned. They are not on our daily calendar. They occur spontaneously with very little warning. We are either sensitive and ready or those moments are lost like feathers cast in the wind.

Being aware of the present time does mean that one must operate with no appreciation of the past or with no planning for the future. To approach life in such a way would be foolish indeed. For a model I turn once again to our Lord.

He certainly had a thoroughgoing respect for the past. His knowledge of history was not just a passing interest. He knew precisely how His life related to the teachings of the prophets. The past was never disregarded as trivial.

The same assertion could undoubtedly be made concerning His forethought and concern for the future. No one could have been more eternally oriented than Jesus. Where would we be today if Jesus had not redeemed our future?

Yet, He never forfeited the joys of the present moment. He knew where the water of life touches the boat—the present moment. The past was never a hitching post, and the future never became a source of frozen anxiety.

I am frustrated and troubled when I observe myself and most of the people that surround me. The cost of our successes require such a high price. We become so wrapped up in the future, the potential for the days to come. And there is so much potential for trouble. Where will I be a year from now? What will be the state of my family? Will I be healthy? Will I have cancer? What if I lose my job? We can become too tied up with things to come that we become numb to what is happening around us. Such a stance toward life is unfortunate for a number of reasons.

For one thing it is dangerous. We worry about people driving under the influence of alcohol and drugs. The problem is that they are not sensitive to conditions around them. Recently, I got in my car and drove from my house to the church office. As I approached the church, it dawned on me that I wasn't going to the church at all. I was supposed to be going to the grocery store, which happened to be in the opposite direction.

This also made me very sad. Look at the good experiences which are overlooked, when one is preoccupied with what happened yesterday or what could happen tomorrow. Time is a precious resource that can only be spent once. There is no recall in reality. When it is done, it is done.

Finally, it is wasteful. We let things go and ignore possibilities for work, pleasure, fun, and service to our Lord. Most of those possibilities are missed not because we seek to do so. We are just unaware of the opportunities of the present moment. We are somewhere else, which is sad indeed.

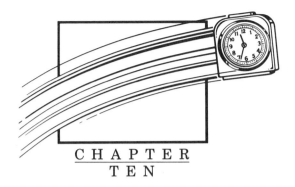

Chasing Happiness

"Fantasy or reality?"

There are few habits in life that "eat away" time and make it pass with greater speed than the temptation to pursue happiness, as if there were a perfect set of circumstances "out there" waiting to be discovered. How easily we can be deluded! Chasing happiness is like trying to "hem up" smoke. Grab a handful of it, and suddenly it is gone. Happiness is the same way, if it is something you are seeking. Happiness is a by-product and not a goal. As a goal, happiness becomes very elusive.

Now, do not hear me saying that there is anything wrong with happiness. Happiness is one of the most precious gifts than anyone could ever hope to possess. Yet, it comes indirectly.

Most of us are convinced that if we could have a few of our dreams come true, then happiness would be a sure thing. But that is not always the case. A young woman in my office was describing her own depression. There were a number of circumstances in her life which, according to her, accounted for her unhappiness. If she could just correct a few things, including a bigger salary, a bigger house, and more social contacts, she would then be able to be happy.

The truth is that these concerns will not guarantee her happiness. If one does not possess some degree of happiness at the moment, happiness may continue to elude the pursuer. Happiness is not an outside quality. It is an inside job. I will be the first to agree that happiness is always easier, when exterior circumstances are satisfactory. But circumstances alone will not guarantee happiness.

The Need for Purpose

My father and I were talking recently over the telephone about how important it is for a person to have a purpose for his or her existence. There must be something that calls us on and motivates us to produce day after day. Unless there is some reason for it all, it just does not make much sense.

As one observes the life of Jesus as He "walks through" the pages of the New Testament, it becomes obvious that He possessed this singleness of purpose for His life. He made it clear to everyone that He had come "to seek and save that which was lost." And it was this purpose in life that allowed Him to move through some terribly troubled times.

That is why He was able to talk with His disciples just hours before the crucifixion about the need for joy in their lives. Knowing that the end of His earthly life was in sight, He told them that He wanted His joy to be in them and their joy to be complete.

Also keep in mind that our Lord wants us to be happy. In His final hours the time was very short. Whenever time is short, minutes become valuable, and we dare not waste a moment. In this kind of moment, when minutes were precious, Jesus chose to talk with them, of all things, about His desire for them to be filled with joy. The timing of His comments underscores His desire for us to be happy. If in your theology you do not think that God wants you to be happy, you need to read the Bible. However, discovering happiness must be a part of our own journey.

This sense of purpose in Jesus' life made all the difference in the world! When things became tough and any normal human being would feel the urge to quit, He remembered the reason for His existence and continued to move forward.

This sense of purpose also kept Jesus from being side tracked into lesser pursuits and wasting His time and energy on things that didn't matter. It was impossible for Him to be pulled off course, because He knew where He was headed. This sense of purpose in life was constantly beckoning Him onward.

Each one of us needs a reason for living, a purpose for our existence. Unfortunately that purpose may not be handed to us on a silver platter; we may have to struggle to discover our purpose. But, if we seek it earnestly, sooner or later we will find it.

Life is, at best, difficult. There must be something that motivates us to stay in the thick of it all. There must be a reason behind our facing each day. Otherwise, we will become the victim of every fad and temptation that comes our way.

Not one of us is here on this earth by mistake. Our existence is no accident. We are a part of the total plan. That belief is crucial for a healthy attitude toward life. And it is just as important that we have a purpose for life. Otherwise, time means very little, and life has no sense of destiny.

What Does Life Mean?

What does life really mean for each of us as individuals? Our personal happiness largely depends on an appropriate answer to that question. Harold Kushner offers a provoking thought:

> Our souls are not hungry for fame, comfort, wealth, or power. Those rewards create almost as many problems as they solve. Our souls are hungry for meaning, for the sense that we have figured out how to live so that our lives matter, so that the world will be at least a little bit different for our having passed through it.[1]

Happiness is a by-product of this meaning in life. Without

it there is no sense of destiny, no backdrop that gives color and depth to the drama of life. Life is in many ways a drama.

Consider the difference that props make to a stage scene. For the last several years my daughter, Melody, has danced a part in the city's annual production of the "Nutcracker." On the night of the dress rehearsal, I sat in the theater and watched the performance. The cast danced as diligently as they could. They gave it their best. But there was something mysteriously lacking. I didn't say anything to Melody, since my knowledge of classical dance is almost nonexistent. Who was I to point out that something was not just right? After all, in the mill village where I grew up a guy would not be caught dead in those tight pants!

The next night was the opening performance, and from the beginning, everything was different. The difference was that the props were in place. There was depth to the stage that was not present during the dress rehearsal.

This sense of purpose and meaning in life becomes the props for our stage. Without them there is no depth to our performance. Kushner once again offers an interesting observation at this point:

> The curator of a butterfly museum in South Wales once introduced me to the "moth with no mouth," a species of caterpillar that lays its eggs and then changes into a moth that has no digestive system.... Nature has designed this moth to reproduce, to lay eggs and pass on the life of the species. Once it has done that, it has no reason to go on living, so it is programmed to die. Are we like that? Do we live only to produce children, to perpetuate the human race?[2]

Our world is full of people who have nearly everything, or so it seems. They have purchased or rented all the cultural creature comforts that have been guaranteed to provide fulfillment to our existence. By all outward appearance, they have it all. Therefore, life should be filled with meaning, or so the market implies.

If that is so, why does suicide, divorce, and general misery continue to increase at alarming rates? Obviously we have been led astray as to the source of happiness in life. One cannot necessarily buy it at the mall.

Where Do We Look?

I was listening recently to a famous musical. The music is beautiful, but the lyrics are profound and get right to the heart of what life really is all about for the character in the song. The music makes me think about some important things.

For example, the old gentleman sings about being happy with nothing. As he sings there seems to be a hint of contentment that almost makes me envious. He obviously does not have much, but what he does have seems to satisfy him. He had a wife who cares, a Lord who loves, and a song in his heart. In addition, he seems to have discovered a secret, whether he realizes it or not. He has become close to what happiness is all about.

Happiness is such an elusive rascal. There is little question that most of us want it. The problem comes in that we just do not know how to find it. My personal feeling is that happiness is not something you seek directly. Happiness tends to be a by-product of one's commitment to the true "basics" of life.

We work ourselves silly to buy, rent, and mortgage happiness. We attempt to find it by trying to possess it and that becomes an endless tunnel. The old gentleman in the song seems to have found it in his gal, his Lord, and his song. And when you get down to the bottom line, isn't that where it is to be found? Most of the other things are simply decorations for the basics of life. Somehow we get sidetracked, and these things, which are a means to an end, become an end in themselves.

The old fellow in the song found it because he knew where to look. I am afraid that most of us are looking in the wrong places. And, while we are looking, time marches on and on.

The Score Card

Several years ago on one of the television talk shows there was a man from Dallas who had made $16 million within the last ten years. This particular guest was quite honest, when asked if he had made enough money. He replied that he intended to keep on making money. He said that, "Life was like a Monopoly game only it used real money, and money was the way the score was kept."

Now, before we become too judgmental and form our pious, church expressions of disapproval, let us be honest and admit that, as we look into the mirror of his statement, we see faint reflections of ourselves. Even for those of us who possess no great wealth, we give away our real feelings and desires by our envy and resentment.

The host asked this particular guest if money made him happy. He sat straight in the chair in which he had been slumped and replied, "Of course not." Then he said that he had many rich friends who were unhappy all of the time. He said also that he knew others who had only the basic essentials of life and were happy. When asked what would make a person happy, he said that three things were essential: something to do, someone to love, and something to look forward to.

Since that time, I have thought a lot about those three essentials for happiness, and I think the man is right on target. I must quickly add that his answer falls short, because he has omitted the central key of Christ, but he is certainly moving in the right direction. For a few minutes let's follow his suggested path to happiness.

Something to Do

First, something to do is certainly a vital part of a meaningful existence. A happy life is one filled with meaningful activity. In the story of the garden of Eden, Adam and Eve were assigned the responsibility of tending the garden. In moments of fatigue, we are tempted to regard paradise as the absence of responsibility. The load sometimes is hard to bear. Yet, the human creature has been fashioned in such a way that meaningful activity is essential to peace of mind. One who has little to do is more susceptible to depression and despair than one who has a sense of calling in life.

Some of the happiest people I know are some of the busiest people I know. While admitting that we can take our "busyness" to an extreme and use it as an escape, happiness is certainly related to purposeful activity. We are made in the image of a creative God. That means we are to derive our joy in similar fashion to our Creator. If God finds meaning in the process of creation, then so will we.

Follow Jesus' ministry through the pages of the New Testament. His life was a ministry of purposeful and sometimes exhausting activity. "Jesus went about all Galilee, teaching in their synagogues, preaching the gospel of the kingdom, and healing all kinds of disease among the people" (Matt. 4:23).

Jesus was not a passive person waiting in some ivory tower for people to approach Him for advice. If you have that kind of image, I would strongly suggest that you read the New Testament. He was a hard working, dynamic individual who knew who He was and what He was about.

The problem with many of us is that we have no sense of overall purpose or direction to the days that make up our time. For too many people today there is nothing that makes them want to get up in the morning. Thomas Carlyle compared human beings with ships. About 75 percent can be compared to ships without rudders. Subject to every shift of wind and tide, they are helplessly adrift. While they fondly hope that one day they'll drift into a rich and successful port, they usually end up on the rocks or run ground.

Too many of us are like the Texan who rushed into the airport and demanded a ticket. "Where to?" asked the agent.

"It doesn't matter," answered the Texan. "I've got business all over."

Happiness comes when we are willing to concentrate on that which is truly important in our lives. This is true of all ages, even retired persons. Retirement does not automatically imply inactivity and no sense of direction.

Someone to Love

In his book, *A Touch of Wonder*, Arthur Gordon tells about his days as a boy scout. He writes,

> I had a troop leader who was an ardent woodsman and naturalist. He would take us on hikes not saying a word, and then challenge us to describe what we had observed: trees, plants, birds, wildlife, everything. Invariably we had not seen a quarter as much as he had, not half enough to satisfy him . . . "Creation is all around," he would cry, waving his arms in vast inclusive circles. "But you're keeping it out. Don't be a buttoned-up person. Stop wearing your raincoat in the shower."[3]

Creation is all around us. Some of us need to stop wearing our raincoat in the shower. He was talking about being open and sensitive to the wonders of creation, and I have known plenty of persons who live in a buttoned-up existence. These persons never really open themselves to love or to be loved.

The challenge is somewhat more difficult for those who have lost most of their family because of age. We must never let our capacity to love die with the passing of our family and friends. Love is the last word. We were created in the image of God whose nature is to love. Because He first loved us, we must find someone to love. Otherwise, our living is like wearing a raincoat in the shower. It is undeniably unsatisfying.

Something to Anticipate

I have developed this thought more fully in the chapter on dreaming, but it is worth repeating here. Too many of us have lost our confidence in life, ourselves, and God, because we have given up our ability to anticipate. We assume that there is nothing to look forward to in life.

We have taken the position of the "preacher" in Ecclesiastes:

> That which has been is what will be,
> That which is done is what will be done,
> And there is nothing new under the sun.
> Is there anything of which it may be said,
> "See, this is new?"
> It has already been in ancient times
> before us (1:9-10).

Difficult times may be the source of our hesitancy to anticipate. Sometimes the routine of life will do it to us. Charlie Brown really was right, when he said: "Happiness is having three things to look forward to and nothing to dread."

We are creatures of habit, and we easily create the habit of just not anticipating anything in life. Our failures will occasionally become our justification for deciding not to anticipate. For many of us it is because we have struck out too many times. You probably already know that Babe Ruth was the world's greatest home-run hitter. What most people don't know is that Babe Ruth set the world's record of strike outs, too. But the Babe is not known for strike outs. He is known for home runs. He obviously was not afraid to anticipate.

An Indirect Goal

There is nothing shameful about wanting to be happy. Happiness is a most honorable goal. But, we must remember that this particular goal comes indirectly. It is a by-product of other pursuits in life. Chase it, and it will elude you like the wind. Set Christlike goals in your life, go for them with all of your might, and you will discover that happiness surrounds you like a beautiful garment.

What does this have to do with time, or even one's perception of time? It has everything to do with it! Our world is full of people who are spending their days and nights chasing happiness only to discover that it is like a mirage. The image is always just ahead, the pool is always dry, and cool water was passed in the path of the mirage. We waste our time and fill our days with frustration, because we don't know what life is all about.

Notes

1. Harold Kushner, *When All You've Ever Wanted Isn't Enough* (New York: Summit Books, 1986), 18.

2. Ibid., 19.

3. Arthur Gordon, *A Touch of Wonder* (Old Tappan, N. J.: Fleming H. Revell, 1974), 60.

Learning to Dream

"The poverty of dreamlessness . . ."

T here is a small plaque on the wall in my father's office that has the following inscription, "A man is never poor as long as he has a dream." My father is also the source of that quote. Even though I remember seeing the plaque many years ago, the words in my recent "middle-aged days" have taken on special significance.

One of the dynamics of the infamous mid-life crisis is the realization that some of our dreams will never come true, and dealing with unrealized dreams is no insignificant matter. One reliable way of avoiding the pain of unrealized dreams is not to dream at all. There are few things in life that pull meaning from our existence more than opting to give up one's dreams. Dreamlessness is a form of poverty.

If we truly want to change our perception of time from the status of enemy to a friend, there must be a place for dreams in our lives. Plenty of reasons can be offered to justify our dreamless lives. We console ourselves by saying that circumstances have robbed us of our dreams. If we no longer dream, it is because we have willingly handed over that quality. The ability to dream is a gift from God. Take away our sense of expectancy, and you have taken away much of what makes us human. Most of us are never more alive than when we have something positive and exciting to anticipate.

My family and I spend a week at the beach each summer.

We all live for that week. For months in advance that vacation week is constantly on my mind. Positive anticipation can move us through a lot of dark days. But, the real dreams of life are much more important than just a week at the beach, although I would settle for that right now!

Of the many capacities that separate us from the lower animals, one of the most important ones is our ability to anticipate and expect. Expectation is what makes many tough days tolerable, and it gives us hope for tomorrow. As long as we have a dream and positive expectations for tomorrow, we can handle today's events with a bit more ease.

However, our capacity "to expect" is very fragile. We may be born with it, but it has to be nurtured or it may be lost. Life takes on a whole new perspective when we lose the ability to have expectations for tomorrow. There are many possibilities which threaten our ability "to expect." Allow me to mention two quickly.

Routine of Life

First, the routine of life may lull us to sleep and cause us to quit expecting anything new or different. After all, isn't every day the same? The truth is that every day is not the same. Each morning is alive with opportunities.

Without a doubt, if life did not have some order or routine to it, we could not tolerate it. But, this does not preclude the emergence of something new that we did not anticipate. The sun will routinely rise tomorrow, but who knows what will follow it?

My wife, Suzanne, enjoys playing the piano, and her music is a regular sound around our home. I can remember in earlier years she would seldom play alone. When Melody was small, she would love to sit by her mother, while Suzanne played the piano. Occasionally, Melody would play along, and strange duets would proceed from the piano. After all, with a name like Melody she is bound to like music.

In the dusty pages of my mind, I remember one morning when Melody was only two or three years old, and she decided to take advantage of the vacant piano bench to do some solo work. I am sure that she thought it would serenade the rest of the family who were just beginning to stir around.

She began to bang on the piano keys and started to sing. The tune was unrecognizable. To her it probably was a beautiful symphony. She was happy, and the words she put to her strange tune were striking. It was striking because she was singing the same word over and over again. For a long time she kept singing, "Today, today, today. . . ." She never changed the lyrics. She appeared to be excited about the fact that it was an early morning and a new day was ahead.

Her concert made me feel a little guilty, because in all honesty, I do not always get up feeling excited about the prospects of a new day. Frequently, I am too anxious about the problems I must face in the next few hours. In my heart I know that a new day is God's gift to an awaiting heart, and we should never take it for granted. How unfortunate that all too often we are anxious about either what happened yesterday or what is going to happen today that we let our anxieties rob us of our excitement.

I will be the first to acknowledge that some of us are just not the kind of folks who feel like turning cartwheels in the early morning. There is supposedly a little gland that acts as a clock for our bodies, and for some, there is a little "squirt" of adrenaline that peps us up for the new day. I am afraid that for some of us that squirt comes later in the morning or maybe not at all. But, even for some of us "not so morning people," that should not keep us from facing a new day with positive anticipation. Time is a gift from God, and it is sad when time becomes a burden instead of the source of joy that God meant it to be.

We may not be able to start the morning with Melody by

singing, "Today, today, today. . . ." But, you have to admit that it is a better routine than most have developed.

Pessimism

A second threat to our ability to expect and dream is the pessimism of our day. Pessimism is a cruel thief. It becomes a habit and can happen to us in quite an unexpecting manner. There are so many people who anticipate absolutely nothing good in the future and their disease can be transmitted like a virus.

Have you ever noticed that when you are around pessimists, you start acting like them?

A Gift to Our Children

There are many lessons that we need to teach our children. One of the most valuable is to teach our children how to dream. Unfortunately, we write dreaming off as an escape from reality and encourage our children to take a more factual approach to reality.

Certainly, dreaming can be an escape, but not always. When used correctly it can guide us and motivate us far beyond our normal limits. Dreaming can be a healthy and positive force in our lives and the lives of our children.

I like what Lou Brock once said, when he was batting .320 and setting new standards for excellence in baseball, "Psychologists say we are the products of our environment. Why can't we be products of our dreams? As long as the obstacles in our lives are not greater than our dreams, we can overcome, grow, and be happy."

It is a fact that successful people are usually the product of dreams. While our environment certainly has its influence upon us, we are much more prone to be shaped by our dreams than our environment.

If we are to dream, why not dream big dreams? We cut ourselves short when we aspire to half of what God intended us to be, to do only a portion of what we could do. We neglect our children's welfare, when we allow them to aspire to only a little of what could be so much more. We have neglected them just as surely as if we had let them play in a busy street.

Needless to say, dreaming can be taken to an extreme. It can be an avoidance of reality, and unrealistic dreaming can set up the conditions for a great deal of frustration. I fear, however, that our problem and that of our children is not aspiring for too much but settling for too little.

From Dreams to Hope

On a much deeper level than just our superficial dreams is a basic dynamic of life called hope. *Hope* is so much more than our dreams for a new car or a house with a pool. *Hope* is the result of a sense of meaning in our lives.

During World War II, a German psychiatrist named Viktor Frankl was imprisoned in a Nazi concentration camp. During those days of horror Dr. Frankl watched everything that was important to him be taken away. His family was executed, and all of his possessions were taken from him, down to the clothes on his back.

It was during these dark days that he began to observe the response of his fellow prisoners. He watched many literally give up and die. Others seemed to move through the death camp experience with a tremendous amount of courage. Frankl began asking the question, "Why do some make it and some do not? Why do some give up and yet others struggle for another day?"

He determined without a doubt that the one irreducible difference was the element of hope. Those who were able to sustain hope were the ones with the best chance of surviving. Once a person quits hoping, he could be "written off." There must be hope for a future and a reason for living, if one is to survive. Without that hope and reason, one becomes vulnerable to any evil force.

Dr. Frankl survived the experience; and being so impressed with the need for hope in life, he established a system of therapy called logotherapy. One of the goals of logotherapy is to generate this element of hope within a person.

With hope for tomorrow humans can survive through life's struggles; without hope, humans are doomed from the start. With a reason to live and hope for tomorrow, one can move through the hard times and good times. Meaning can be found in the suffering that surrounds us. Even as one moves through the "valley of the shadow of death," there is strength to move forward. Hope is vital to living. Time becomes empty when there is no hope.

Where is this hope to be found? I can speak only for myself. There is an old hymn that echoes the essence of meaning and hope.

> My hope is built on nothing less
> Than Jesus' blood and righteousness;
> I dare not trust the sweetest frame,
> But wholly lean on Jesus' name.
> On Christ, the solid Rock, I stand;
> All other ground is sinking sand,
> All other ground is sinking sand.[1]

Note

1. Edward Mote, "The Solid Rock," No. 337, *Baptist Hymnal*, (Nashville: Convention Press, 1975).

The Real Measure
of Time

"How old was he?"

H ave you noticed that whenever we hear of the death of someone we frequently ask about his or her age? After hearing the news of the death of a friend's parent, our first question will recurrently be, "How old was she?" When a friend's work associate dies, sooner or later we get around to asking, "How old was he?"

Perhaps one reason we ask that question is we feel we can more easily justify the death of someone who is more advanced in years. If one has accumulated enough years we can more easily accept one's death and assume it to be a natural event. Death seems less tragic, when we can say they had a "full life."

The concern for one's age is obviously a result from our tendency to measure one's life in years, as if that were the sole gauge. Strange as it may sound, the duration of human life depends largely on how it is measured. Now is the time to give consideration to the way we measure life rather than in retrospect as we "close the books."

The psalmist stated, "The days of our years are seventy years" (Ps. 90:10). In doing so the Psalmist has only given us a description of life's expectancy. It is obviously not a guarantee of that many years. We can all name persons who never came close to that age, and we can think of some who have far exceeded that number. The Psalmist was simply saying that the average life expectancy is seventy years and, even then, when compared to God these years are but a sigh. Yet, much depends on how we measure life. What are some possibilities?

First, one's life can obviously be measured in years, and certainly that is the natural thing to do. There is no shame in accumulation of time. One half of all born in the world die in infancy and childhood. Of those who reach ten, only two out of five reach seventy. One in a hundred reaches ninety, and one in a hundred thousand lives a full century.

With the advances in medical science the duration of human life is becoming longer. Early detection of disease and scientific methods of treatment have not only added length to a person's life but in some cases quality as well. Yet, our mortal bodies remain subject to stress and age; and we, therefore, must continue to deal with the fact that time runs out.

Dr. Carlyle Marney once began a sermon by looking over his congregation and saying, "What a bunch of losers!" He was not referring to them with reference to failing. What he was referring to was the fact that for each of us time sooner or later runs out. Is that not what death is all about? Time eventually runs out. There are, however, some other ways of measuring life.

Accomplishments

Consider the accomplishments of an individual. Some people do far more with a few years than many do with a large number. A life especially worth celebrating is one who combines numbers of years and accomplishments. Keep in mind that life's true accomplishments are not always the ones which appear in the newspaper headlines. Most great acts of love go unnoticed by the masses. In fact, many labors of love are known only by God.

Unfortunate is the fact that the normal measure of a life puts quantity over quality. Consider the life of our Lord. You cannot question the quality of His life, and His work was done in a small number of years. The quality of one's life is remembered long after the quantity has been forgotten.

Circumstances

Some lives are remembered only in terms of the circumstances under which they lived. Consider, however, the circumstances of our lives today. Just think of the changes that have occurred during the span of our lives. From the walking on the moon to the unbelievable advances in science. So much has changed. In science, world events, and culture there is little about our world that is the same as when we were young.

But we must keep in mind that most changes in circumstances occur beyond our control. We may have little to do with the events that define our lives. While we may be remembered for having lived in a certain era of history, we can claim little credit for it.

Preparation

Another important measure that we should never forget has to do with the issue of preparation. I can describe it best by sharing an experience I recently had with a friend.

I was visiting Mary Robinson in the hospital. She is a member of my congregation who had just received the report that several arteries in her heart were blocked. Surgery would be required. As you might expect, this information came rather suddenly and was greeted with a certain amount of shock.

Mary and I talked about this surgery which had been suddenly scheduled for the next day. There is no such thing as routine surgery, especially concerning the heart; but Mary had a calm sense of confidence that came from deep within her. Mary and I have been friends for a number of years, and I have come to know and appreciate her strong faith. She spoke freely and with little emotion about the possibilities of the surgery. She said almost as matter of fact, "If it is time for the Lord to take me, then so be it. I have no fear of dying. I have spent a lifetime preparing for this moment, and I am very much at peace with the possibilities." I did not even comment for nothing else needed to be said. I nodded in total agreement.

Our most important measure is at the point of preparation for life to come. In fact, the best way to live this life is in preparation for the life to follow. One lives best who early chooses the only true foundation for life. All other measures become insignificant in comparison with this characteristic.

Preparation for life beyond is a lifelong process. It is not meant to be a crash course in eternal survival taken at the last minute. The preparation begins the moment one opens himself or herself to salvation through Christ. Preparation continues through all of one's days. The beauty of this measure is that when that moment of death comes in the history of each one of us, the event becomes a simple transition.

The writer of Revelation stated it well, "Blessed are those who do His commandments, that they may have the right to the tree of life, and may enter through the gates into the city" (Rev. 22:14).

Both the Psalmist and the writer of Revelation described the essence of our mortal life. Time can be measured in many different kinds of ways. But, the best measure I know is found in the process of preparation. One's entire life can become a time of preparation. When that is the case, death really does become only a transition, a movement from one stage to another. Time then is expanded. Life becomes no longer confined.

I'm going to take all the years God gives me. I will love

and appreciate every one of them. However, I hope that quantity does not become the sole measure of my life. With just a little forethought I can plan for something more than the end of life.

The Price
of Complexity

"Needs made complicated . . ."

It's Saturday night, and I am absolutely exhausted. I have spent the entire day doing the things that are supposedly necessary to keep the wheels of domestic life turning. There were a few minor automobile repairs that had to be completed. There were some problems with several household appliances. We had to make a trip to the mall for a couple of items. The lawn had to be mowed; straw swept from the roof; a gutter cleaned out; and a number of other things done just to meet current needs. All of these things had to be done today, because there is no other free time during the week. It was today or not at all.

I now sit in my study and, exhausted or not, must do some "fine tuning" on three different sermons which I must preach tomorrow. At the moment, however, my mind keeps wandering toward a brief verse in Ecclesiastes where the writer says, "God made man simple; man's complex problems are of his own devising" (7:29, author). His statement is more than descriptive. It is an indictment of our modern life-style.

The writer of Ecclesiastes, who lived long before our modern-day pace, was right on target. In looking back over my day, I realize that the majority of the demands that have fallen upon me today are a result of my own doing. Most of my activity was performed in the infamous pursuit of happiness. The problem is that the requirements for happiness today seem almost overwhelming. It takes so much, and the result is a complex life-style that exists for the purpose of keeping us moving along in the process.

Too many of us live our days in bondage to all the things that we assume are necessary to keep us happy. It takes so much that the inevitable result is a tremendous amount of complexity "that follows us all the days of our life." We live in a country that was born out of the human desire to be free, but we have developed life-styles that have enslaved us. It is no wonder that time seems to fly when we are having fun, and even when we're not. The reason is that we have created so many needs that ultimately have little to do with the bottom line of happiness in our lives. The cost of meeting those needs is high in terms of time. Not only does "time fly" but we are so tired that little joy can be found in God's creation.

Generalizations can be risky, but it appears to me that most of us are operating with little joy in our lives. We seem so overwhelmed by routine demands that joy is just a sweet memory, or maybe something we have only read about in the Bible. That loss of joy can be attributed to many things, but I lift one possibility before you at this point. The bottom line is that it takes too much to make us happy.

Real Needs

The psalmist depicts God's creation of humanity as the climax of all that He created. "You have made him a little lower than the angels, And You have crowned him with glory and honor" (Ps. 8:5). We are created in the image of God, who is the source of joy. Therefore, created within us is the potential and capacity for joy and peace. The assumption is that this capacity is realized as a person goes through the process of having his or her needs met, which raises a real question. What are our real needs? It is at this point that I see most of us becoming helpless victims of a highly technical and powerful marketing science. While we were fearful of "Big Brother" controlling our lives, another giant has slipped up in the dark.

Our needs are relatively simple. God created us with certain needs for food, shelter, clothing, intimacy, and relationships. He has provided some simple ways of meeting these needs. Such was the case for His first human models, and the present line of human production has changed little since those first models.

During the process of the years, we have fabricated all kinds of other needs and have allowed ourselves to submit to a giant that has changed every aspect of our lives. Not only has the giant changed life, but now is in control. Call the giant whatever you like, advertising, marketing, conformity, greed, or just a general dissatisfaction with one's basic self; the game it plays is tragic indeed.

We have needs; and if we play the game, we believe that we can satisfy all our needs. Therefore, we work, buy, and borrow. Meanwhile, in order to increase its power over us, the giant increases our needs. Part of the game is that it tightens its demand for conformity. Thus, one becomes all the more committed to the illusion that the giant holds before us, while we become hopelessly mortgaged to play the game.

Irresistible Images

How does all this happen? The giant informs us and shapes us by pointing us toward its definition of happiness by presenting us with irresistible images of ourselves that are so perfect that no one would possibly have doubt. The presentation of the "good life" is so convincing that one is no longer even remotely aware that it might change into something less satisfying.

In practice, expensive fun often blossoms into another full blown need, which then calls for a still more costly refinement of satisfaction, which again fails us. The end of the cycle is despair, or rather bankruptcy.

There is certainly nothing immoral about purchasing nice things or improving one's personal state. The real test comes at the point of who is in control. Do we truly control our lives or does the giant? The giant is alive and well and working day and night for new ways of presenting irresistible images to drive, wear, eat, abide, recreate, rest, and sleep in certain ways. These ways are guaranteed to take one to the peak of fulfillment. In the end, life, which was designed to be simple, has become complex.

The game of the giant in itself is not immoral. However, these futile promises have made us prisoners of a process and our capacities for joy, peace, and truth are never liberated. That is not only immoral but tragic.

Remember the words of Jesus: "Consider the lilies, how they grow: they neither toil nor spin; and yet I say to you, even Solomon in all his glory was not arrayed like one of these" (Luke 12:27). The implications of Jesus' teaching are unlimited. One clear message is that God is aware of our basic needs and seeks to provide for their satisfaction. The problem is that we have nursed our needs until they demand more than we can comfortably provide.

One reason that "time flies" is that the needs of our lives have become so demanding that we are slaves to their satisfaction. As a result one might say, "Wise is the man who learns to think for himself, guided no longer by the systems designed to create artificial needs and then satisfy them." Simplicity frees us. Duplicity wraps chains around our souls.

The bottom line is that it takes too much to make us happy. In order to keep the "pump" operating, we must overextend ourselves and sooner or later we run dry. The truth is we have no one to blame but ourselves. We would be surprised to discover just how simple our needs really are. Most of what we think is necessary really isn't necessary after all. Even if days could be lengthened, time would still fly because of the pace we keep. Consider also that amount of anxiety which is another consequence of our life-style.

There is no quick fix to our problem, because it is a problem of life-style. Life-style can be translated as habits, and habits are hard to change. Honesty and courage are two requirements, if change is to ever occur. The problem is that the root causes of our complex life-style get close to where we live, too close.

Priorities

A part of our problem is that we want it all. We are bombarded from every direction about all the things that are supposed to add meaning to life for us. Life for us is like a child going into a toy store decorated for Christmas. Everything looks so good. He wants it all. His sensory system becomes overloaded as he imagines life with all that is before his eyes.

The truth is that we can't have it all. Even if we could afford it, time and circumstances would still not allow it. We must still establish some priorities in life. Otherwise, we only move from one fad to another, and anxiety is usually the result. Just think of the anxiety we experience as we try to make certain no one takes our things from us.

Richard J. Foster in writing about the discipline of simplicity offers some good advice. He suggests that freedom from anxiety is characterized by three inner attitudes. "If what we have we receive as a gift, and if what we have is to be cared for by God, and if what we have is available to others, then we will possess freedom from anxiety. This is the inward reality of simplicity."[1]

First, we should recognize that what we have is a gift from

God. The temptation is great and quite natural to assume that our possessions are a direct result of our hard work. Work is part and parcel to our human existence, but the product of our labor can never be separated from the grace of God. An accident or misfortune quickly reminds us how radically dependent we are on sources outside ourselves for everything. We are dependent upon God for our daily bread, whether we want to admit it or not.

Second, we should grant God the opportunity to care for what He has provided. God is more than capable of protecting what we seemingly possess. Once again, the issue is whether we actually trust God. Does this mean that we have the right to be negligent? Of course not! Christian maturity is never to be sought at the expense of common sense.

The third inner attitude involves making our things available to other people. This attitude is quite difficult to develop because of our fear of the future. The temptation is great for us to cling to our possessions because of our anxiety about tomorrow. If we knew that after our goods were shared there would still be adequate resources for the future, our anxieties would be considerably less. To truly believe in God as the One who ultimately provides will encourage us to share, because we know He will care for us.

In spite of what we see on television and at the movies, we cannot have it all. There is neither time, energy, or money. To ignore that truth will set time at warp speed.

A Guiding Principle

Even after one has established some sense of priority in life, there must be a guiding principle in the center. We are always taking our cues from something or someone. Who or what that might be is of extreme importance.

In a superbly written book entitled *God's Joyful Surprise,* Sue Monk Kidd deals with this issue. She says, "A center is not simply an inner place where you are in touch with God's presence. Most important, it is a space from which you can focus your entire life. Being centered is not so much a state of being as a point of beginning."[2]

This is accomplished by refocusing our attention on God. Most of us keep God on the periphery of our lives rather than in the center. The secret is to be found by granting attention to God in all that we think and do. The more that we are aware of His presence in our lives, the more we are willing to shape our existence around Him.

Our lives will invariably have some kind of guiding principle. Even for the believer, God is not the only possibility for our center.

The Painful Truth

The real truth underlying much of our frantic life-style which in turn eats away our days and nights is a dynamic called greed. We want all we can get; and, as soon as we can get it, we don't want anybody else to share it. Greed is certainly not anything new. Human beings have been familiar with it since the garden of Eden, and greed is alive today. It constantly keeps us in trouble as well as complicating our lives.

Sometimes while my family is eating the evening meal the television will be on in the next room where it can be seen from the table. It is usually the time when a popular game show is on. I am intrigued by how many times greed causes a contestant to lose it all. They will have accumulated a fair sum of money, and the answer to the puzzle is obvious. They must either solve the puzzle and keep their earnings, or spin again with the hope of increasing their sum. So many times they will select to spin again. You can see the anxiety in their faces as they watch the wheel turn. Frequently, the wheel stops on "bankrupt," and they lose everything. They lost it all, because they were not satisfied with what they had and wanted more. The truth is that we do the same thing to ourselves every day.

Our Lord has some strong things to say about the person whose only goal in life was to build bigger barns. We like to skip right over that parable, because it hits too close to home. We are basically greedy people. We want it all, and we want it now. As a result, our days are never long enough. Time flies.

Notes

1. Richard J. Foster, *The Celebration of Discipline* (New York: Harper and Row, 1978), 77.

2. Sue Monk Kidd, *God's Joyful Surprise* (New York: Guideposts, 1987), 60.

CHAPTER
FOURTEEN

The Celebrating
of Time

"Tying together loose ends . . ."

O ne of my favorite movies of all time is *Fiddler on the Roof.* Interestingly enough, my appreciation of the movie has grown over the years, and for an obvious reason. When I saw the movie for the first time, Suzanne and I had one child, a baby boy. And at that point in time, I had the feeling that he would always be a helpless infant who needed someone to look after him day and night.

Since that first occasion, I have seen the movie numerous times, including a stage production. The last time was as recent as a few weeks ago. Much has changed during that span of time. We now have two children. The one who was an infant, in constant need, is now in college and needs very little from us, except a regular audit of his checking account. Little explanation is required to understand why I can now so easily identify with Tevye who watches all types of change embrace his family. The changes are not necessarily bad, but they are changes just the same.

While this story deals with a number of issues, some religious and some historical, the story becomes a case study of time and its impact upon a community, and more specifically upon a family. Tevye appears on the surface to be a helpless victim of time.

He has dreams for his family, like any father. He has a

relatively clear expectation of what the future will bring. And yet, one by one, his children chart courses that are foreign to his expectations. Not only does time change his children, but the future becomes radically different than he would dare have expected.

With all of the surprises that come his way, what keeps it all together for him? To answer that question one must go back to the early moments of the movie to the scene of the fiddler on the crest of the roof. A child who observes the fiddler raises a legitimate question, "What keeps the fiddler from falling?"

The question is immediately answered by the singing of the chorus, "Tradition!" The film makes a good pitch for tradition and strongly suggests that tradition is the dynamic that provides the balance to keep him from falling.

What, therefore, keeps Tevye from loosing his balance when one change after another is hurled at him? Tradition is the answer as well. Tevye says that we are all like a fiddler on the roof trying to scratch out a pleasant living without losing our balance.

One must keep in mind that tradition is more than a lot of useless ritual and meaningless activity. Webster defines *tradition* as the passing down of elements of a culture from generation to generation or any time honored set of practices. We usually think in terms of activities. Activity may be involved, but the essence of tradition is the intent to link pieces of life together in such a way that some sense of meaning comes from the total picture.

A Simple Pause

One particular dynamic that was such an important part of Tevye's tradition and life-style was the simple practice of celebration. They were not afraid to celebrate. Those special moments when the passage of one stage to another took place were greeted with celebration. Celebrating seems to make a lot more sense than mourning. This is not to say that grief does not play an important role in our life.

Grief is the natural way of dealing with loss. But, grief should not be our primary way of approaching life in general. Grief is a part of our common experience as well, but celebration is a way of openly approaching the inevitable changes in life and saying, "Yes, come on. I'm ready." One may opt to fight the inevitable with tears of grief, but an open and willing stance makes more sense.

Webster defines *celebration* as observing with ceremonies of respect or festivity. I like that attitude toward life. One can fight it at every stage or celebrate it. We must choose.

Celebration is more than meaningless noise and shallow laughter. True celebration is much deeper, more central, more powerful, and inherently more of a Christian function than we sometimes realize.

The second chapter of John has a beautiful description of Jesus' participation at the wedding feast in Cana of Galilee.

> Jesus was invited to the wedding and so were His disciples. When the wine had run short, Jesus' mother said to Him, "They have no wine."
>
> Jesus said to her, "Lady, let me handle this in my own way. My hour has not yet come."
>
> His mother said to the servants, "Do whatever He tells you to do."
>
> There were six stone water pots standing there, six for the Jewish purifying customs and each of them held about twenty or thirty gallons. Jesus said to them, "Fill the water pots with water." They filled them up to the very brim. He said to them, "Draw from them now, and take what you draw to the steward in charge." They did so.
>
> When the steward had tasted the water which had become wine, he did not know where it came from, but the servants who had drawn the water knew. The steward called the bridegroom and said, "Everyone first sets before the guests

the good wine, and then, when they have drunk their fill, he sets before them the inferior wine. You have kept the good wine until now."

Jesus did the first of His signs in Cana of Galilee, and displayed His glory; and His disciples believed on Him (vv. 2-11, author).

In so doing, Jesus did more than perform His first miracle. He affirmed the importance of celebration. While Scripture does not say so, one can easily assume that Jesus was glad to be at the wedding celebration. One might also easily imagine the disciples saying to Jesus, "We are entirely too busy to attend some silly wedding. There are more important things we must do."

Can you not hear Jesus saying to His disciples, "Those duties will still be there when we finish. There are other things which add meaning to those duties. We must go to the wedding."

It is no accident that John records Jesus' first miracle at this wedding feast. It was a time of joy and laughter, but most of all it was celebration.

How can celebration become truly a Christian experience? Celebration is not just a lot of noise and commotion or a short-lived pep rally. Instead, it is something that takes place within. It may very well be a quiet exercise. It can happen in a silent moment of the night, on a mountain top, in one's backyard, at the breakfast table, or at an exhilarating moment of worship in a stain-glass sanctuary.

Celebration is a claiming of the past, a recognition of the present, and an open stance toward the future. It occurs when we thank God for the past as we see now more clearly His hand upon our life. It occurs when we claim the present moment as a sacred gift—the only moment that we can truly bear influence upon our surroundings. It occurs when we position ourselves in such a way that the future becomes our friend, not an enemy.

Celebration is an exercise that connects that "which was" with that "which will be." Celebration is more than just recognizing another passage of life. It is embracing the present moment and holding to it just as Jacob wrestled with God and would not let Him go until God gave him His blessing. Celebration occurs at its best when we lift a moment in time before God and ask for His blessing. With His blessing upon it that moment is suddenly released from the influence of time.

Celebration is an act of faith. It is the process of walking through a door. It is the closing of one door and the opening of another. It is the end of one stage and the beginning of another. It is saying good-bye and at the same time saying hello. After all, is not life best understood as a lot of good-byes and hellos? It is an act of faith in God when we realize that for every good-bye there is a hello.

We need something to connect the past with the future. We do so by thanking God for the past that has brought us to this point in time and for a future that makes sense only when connected to the past. Both are gifts from God and are claimed by celebrating the *present moment.*

One essential component of celebration is thanksgiving. Without a sense of thanksgiving, celebration has no meaning. Celebration is not just a casual recognition service. It is a temporary pause in the routine rush when one lifts before God a moment in time and from the depths of the soul one says, "Thank You, God."

The point we often forget is that celebration has both horizontal and vertical dimension. There is the horizontal dynamic of connecting the past and the future. Just as importantly, there is the vertical dimension of connecting the moment in time with God.

Rejoice

The apostle Paul reminds us to "rejoice in the Lord always. Again I will say, rejoice!" (Phil. 4:4). Since Paul seemed to prefer the word *rejoice*, let's follow his thinking for a moment. To "rejoice in the Lord" does not mean that one is to be insensitive to the sorrows of one's own life nor the sufferings of the world. It does mean that these dark realities will not be allowed to become the master of life or completely overwhelm the sunshine that also is a part of life.

Faith in Christ and obedience to Him are sources of this joy. Disconnect one's celebrating from one's faith and the system falls apart. Consider Paul's circumstance for a moment. When he instructs us to rejoice, he does so with the knowledge that death is not far away. Yet, he still says to rejoice. How can one possibly think of joy or celebration in the shadow of death?

Surely he was not completely independent of these circumstances. But, they were not the ground of his joy. Even in a moment which was far less than perfect, he could connect the present with the presence of God and celebrate.

Richard Foster touches this issue when he says, "The spirit of celebration will not be in us until we have learned to be 'careful for nothing.' And we will never have a carefree indifference to things until we totally trust God."[1]

Interestingly, Paul went on to help us understand how this joy-filled celebration takes place. His wise word of counsel was not to be anxious. Paul was not the first to speak in such terms. Jesus said, " 'Do not be worry about your life, . . . what you shall put on' " (Matt. 6:25). Such freedom from care does not come naturally. That is why celebration must have a vertical dimension, or it never really takes place. When we truly celebrate a moment in God's presence, He not only blesses that moment but redeems it as well.

There is one other point that Foster makes in his classic book that is worthy of repeating.

> Far and away the most important benefit of celebration is that it saves us from taking ourselves too seriously . . . . Of all people we (Christians) should be the most free, alive, interesting. Celebration adds a note of gaiety, festivity, hilarity to our lives. After all, Jesus rejoiced so fully in life that He was accused of being a wine-bibber and glutton.

Foster adds that most of us lead such sour lives that we could never be accused of such things.[2]

Celebration gives us a perspective on life that is essential to happiness and gives meaning to the passing of time. To quote Foster once again, "In celebration the high and the mighty regain their balance and the weak and lowly receive new stature. Who can be high or low at the festival of God? Together the rich and the poor, the powerful and the powerless all celebrate the glory and wonder of God. There is no leveler of caste systems like festivity."[3]

Celebration occurs when we thank God for the past as we see His hand upon our life more clearly. It occurs when we claim the present moment as a sacred gift, the only moment in which we can influence life. It occurs when we position ourselves in such a way that the future becomes our friend, not an enemy.

The beauty of it all is that more than just the future becomes our friend. Without realizing it, a "cease-fire" is quietly declared on time in general. "Rejoice in the Lord always. Again I will say, rejoice!" Could it be that Paul discovered something that most of us have ignored or at least forgotten? Maybe we should listen. Better yet, maybe we should celebrate! That includes the big things and little things. We can do it alone or with other people.

An evening meal can become a special time of joy. There can be genuine celebration for safekeeping throughout the day. Today is done; tomorrow is a new opportunity. Birthdays are more than just cake and ice cream. The past is lifted up, and thanks offered. A new year is anticipated with joy.

A morning walk becomes a moment of worship. Centuries have produced all within sight. God continues to create. You are a part of that moment and the creation. That's cause for celebration. At bedtime, there comes a special hug from a child who still has the clean smell of her evening bath. Years have been invested in that hug, and they are only going to become sweeter and better. Time to celebrate!

The hymn is not just any old hymn. It was a favorite of a grandparent who has been dead for many years. Lots of good memories come to mind, and you carry those influences into the future. Thank God for special people. Time to celebrate!

Routine chores are finally done. Tomorrow they must be done again. But, it is for a good cause. They are for people that are gifts from God. Such chores are never routine. Time to celebrate!

Then there are anniversaries, holidays, and special events. The opportunities for celebration are unlimited. They are simple times when one stops, lifts the present moment before God, and offers a heartfelt thank you. In so doing you recognize that the future is out there, something to be anticipated. Tradition not only keeps us from falling off the roof, but it surely does tie up a lot of loose ends!

Notes

1. Richard J. Foster, *Celebration of Discipline* (New York: Harper and Row, 1978), 167.

2. Ibid., 168.

3. Ibid.

Learning to Wait

"It's never been easy . . ."

I must confess that there are few issues that influence my perception of time more than the dynamic of waiting. Patience has never been my long suit. I do not like to wait on anything. That is not bragging, just a fact.

The issue of patience is much more than just a personality problem with which I struggle. It also is an intensely personal issue of faith. I have positive feelings about the power of prayer. I strongly believe that God not only listens to our prayers but also answers them. In fact, there are few things in life that I am more certain about than the influence of our prayers. My problem is that God does not always work on my schedule.

The story is told of little Benjamin who sat down to write a letter to God for a little sister. He started the letter: "Dear God, I've been a very good boy . . ." He stopped, thinking, *No, God won't believe that.* He wadded up the paper, threw it away, and started again.

"Dear God, most of the time I've been a good boy . . ." He stopped in the middle of the line, again thinking, *God won't be moved by this,* so into the trash can went the wad of paper.

Benjamin went into the bathroom, grabbed a big terry-cloth towel off the bar, brought it into the living room, and laid it on the couch. Then he went to the fireplace mantle, reached up, and brought down a statue of the Madonna, the mother of Jesus, that he had eyed many times.

Benjamin placed the statue in the middle of the towel, gently folded over the edges, and placed a rubber band around the whole thing. He brought it to the table, took another piece of paper, and began writing his third letter to God: "Dear God, If you ever want to see your mother again . . ."[1]

We have all been there. We want God to give us patience, and we want Him to give it to us right now! We are intelligent creatures and know what we want! We know what is best and deserve it pronto. If time is to ever be our friend, we must have a better knowledge of the theological implications of waiting.

No New Problem

Paul made an interesting reference to this issue in his letter to the church at Corinth. He reminded them to be careful about their witness. "So that you come short in no gift, eagerly waiting for the revelation of our Lord Jesus Christ" (1 Cor. 1:7).

Paul was referring to a problem that was developing in that early church. Those early members wanted Christ to come back for them. He said He would return, and they wanted it to happen now. They were facing some serious problems in that community as they sought to be good witnesses. Their confident hope was that some day Christ would return and their faithfulness would be rewarded. In the meantime they were involved in a process that we all know in one way or another, something called waiting.

Unfortunately, I am afraid that too few people today are anxiously awaiting the return of our Lord. We would all do better if there were more interest in that day. Even our perception of time would be radically affected by a more lively anticipation of that day. We experience our struggle with waiting in other ways as well.

To be honest, I don't like to wait for anything. Lines at the bank, grocery store, and tag office stretch my patience to the very limits. Consider the time we wait at traffic lights. I actually calculated once how much time I spent at traffic lights in the course of one year. I felt like I had tossed a big portion of my life in the flowing river, and there was no return.

I have heard the testimonies of other people who have struggled with traffic problems and red lights. Some have used it for memorizing Scripture, singing new songs, and even praying. I think those are commendable ways of filling that time, but I have never done well with any of those approaches. It seems a little like throwing in the towel and giving approval to waiting. I don't like to wait.

One use of that time happened to me recently, but I would not recommend it. I had been up late for several nights and was tired. I was going from the church to the hospital, and the light in front of the hospital was red. The next thing I knew horns were blowing all around me, since I had traffic blocked. I had gone to sleep waiting on the red light. Fortunately, my foot was on the brake pedal, and I had remained in one place. Naps are special moments of rest but not to be taken at a major intersection.

An Intense Issue of Faith

My biggest struggle with waiting is not at red lights but in terms of matters of life and faith. The Bible tells us to be persistent and that we should pray with a sense of expectation. The problem is that God does not always work on our schedule.

In a certain orchestra number by Joseph Haydn, the flute player is supposed to sit quietly for seventy-four measures and then come in exactly on the upbeat of the seventy-fifth.

To me Haydn was asking a lot for someone to do this. To expect a musician to wait that patiently and perform that precisely is looking for a rare individual.

In a similar way it is a rare person of faith who can wait patiently on God without some sense of struggle. As one writer has said, "I need to take a lesson in patience. Do you know where I can take a crash course?" For our common struggle with difficulty in waiting, allow me to suggest three qualities that are a part of a healthy attitude toward waiting.

First, *humility* is a vital component of a healthy willingness to wait. The problem with waiting is that when we are doing it, there are some things that are not under our control. To wait means that we are not masters of our circumstances. In spite of diligence, hard work, and ability, there are some things that we cannot control or hurry.

Shakespeare said, "How poor are they that have no patience. What wound did ever heal but by degrees?" We all feel like Phillips Brooks who was pacing back and forth one day and a friend asked him what was wrong. Brooks said, "I'm in a hurry, but God is not!" We've all been there.

Humility means that we must recognize who we are and that we are limited creatures. It means that our schedule does not fuel the universe and determine the timing of the planets. Humility means not only recognizing who we are but who God is. It means that God has a schedule that supersedes our own.

Children will frequently do better than adults. I like the story of the little boy standing at the bottom of a department store escalator. Intently looking at the handrail, the small boy would not take his eyes away. A salesperson asked, "Are you lost?"

"No." came the reply, "I'm waiting for my chewing gum to come back."

Humility means waiting like a child and saying, "There

are some things in life that I cannot control." It definitely takes humility to wait.

Second, *faith* is an irreplaceable component of waiting. If waiting means that we are not in control of things, then we must develop some peace with the fact there is One who is in control. On an intellectual level most of us have accepted that fact, but on a practical level we have a lot of work to do.

The Psalmist offerred a word of advice for the impatient waiter: "Trust in the Lord, and do good; Dwell in the land, and feed on His faithfulness. Delight yourself also in the Lord, And He shall give you the desires of your heart" (37:3-4).

The story is told of George MacDonald who failed as a parish minister. In frustration he became a writer. For years he wrote with only modest success. But finally, his skill as a writer of fantasies, children stories, and poetry won him success. He became one of the best known English writers of his time. In fact, one of MacDonald's books gave C. S. Lewis his first image of Christianity, and Lewis become one of the most influential Christian writers of all times. MacDonald once said, "The principal part of faith is patience."

Third, we need to realize that waiting is not just a passive time loss. Waiting can become a *creative strategy*. Times of waiting can become some of God's best opportunities to establish direction and meaning for our lives. As we step back from the daily frantic pace, we often gain a perspective on life that is totally impossible while we are running in little circles. Strategies become visible to us that make the difference between success and failure.

Something You Do

Two years ago, I wrote a book entitled *Hurry Up and Rest*. In the book I proposed that rest was not passive but rather something that you do. Genuine rest is a process that involves one mentally, physiologically, emotionally, and spiritually. It is something that you do intentionally, not passive inactivity. The same can be said about waiting. When it is perceived positively, waiting becomes not only a time of "realignment" but a basis of hope.

Patt Barnes in *Guideposts* tells the story of a pastor on the day after Easter pausing at the top of the steps which lead from the church to the city street. The street was crowded, and people were rushing to their jobs. Sitting in her usual place inside a small archway was an old flower lady. At her feet were corsages and boutonnieres on a newspaper. The flower lady was smiling, her wrinkled face was alive with joy.

The pastor started down the stairs, then on an impulse turned and picked out a flower. As he put it in his lapel, he said, "You look happy this morning."

"Why not? Everything is good." she said.

She was dressed shabbily and seemed very old that her reply startled him. "No troubles?" he responded.

"You can't reach my age and not have troubles," she replied. "Only it's like Jesus and Good Friday." She paused for a moment.

"Yes?" prompted the pastor.

"Well, when Jesus was crucified on Good Friday, that was the worst day for the whole world. When I get troubles, I remember that. Then I think what happened only three days later—Easter and our Lord arising. So when I get troubles, I've learned to wait three days, and somehow everything gets all right again," she smiled and said good-bye.

The old woman may not have had a position of great importance, but her wisdom surpasses the world's great scholars. "Give God a chance to work and wait three days." Such an attitude might save us a few wrinkles on our own brow.[2] An anonymous poet wrote:

There is a voice, "a still, small voice" of love,
Heard from above;
But not amidst the din of earthly sounds,
Which here confounds;
By those withdrawn apart it best is heard,
And peace, sweet peace, breathes in each gentle word.

The Psalmist wrote, "Wait on the Lord; Be of good courage, And He shall strengthen your heart; Wait, I say, on the Lord!" (27:14).

Waiting Can Be a Blessing

There is a certain perspective of life that comes to us only when we are willing to back away from the tireless circles in which we move. I am not implying that activity is not important. Accomplishments come only through the expending of energy, and there is no praise for laziness.

Because of forced waiting we separate ourselves from those things that draw from us, and we discover a special kind of strength. There is a need within each one of us to seek for a time to search our conscience and think on the benefits of God. If we can withdraw ourselves from unprofitable running about, from the hearing of rumors and vain tales, and from endless anxiety, we will find that special time to be occupied in holy meditations.

History is full of holy men and women who found the necessity to regularly flee worldly living and make their choice to serve God in the secret of their heart. It is in silence and the quietness of heart that we discover ourselves and the God who created us. Moments when we are forced to wait can become our best friend.

There is little question that we live in a noisy world, and much of the noise is necessary to our way of life. There must be times, however, when we retire from that noise and let our spirits catch up with our bodies. Otherwise, we feel separated from ourselves and from our Creator.

If Jesus needed times of silence and withdrawal, how much more do we mortals need to do the same? There are times when we feel that God is far away, that there is great distance between us. The distance is not a problem with God, but rather within ourselves. God is always closer than our breath. The problem is that we are too busy to notice.

There is indeed a perspective of life that comes to us, when we are willing to back away and allow peace a proper place in our hearts. This perspective will not always happen in the rush of the world. So, I am convinced that God in His wisdom knows that we just need to do a little waiting, and suddenly we are in an enormous traffic jam. It never really occurred to me before that a traffic jam could have a theological dimension to it. That may take a little getting used to!

Notes

1. *Parables, Etc.*, vol. 10, no. 2 (Plattville, Colo.: Saratoga Press, 1990).

2. Adapted with permission from *Guidepost* Magazine © 1988 by Guidepost Associate, Inc. Carmel, NY, 10512.

Above and Beyond

"Trust is the key . . ."

T he process of changing one's perception of time from enemy to friend is not an easy task. There is no quick fix to
"making friends" with time. At best it is a pilgrimage that
requires honesty on one hand and resourcefulness on the
other. This pilgrimage involves us emotionally, mentally,
physically, and spiritually.

The journey requires more than just learning new ways to
measure time. One must understand that time, as por-
trayed in the Bible, is going somewhere; there is movement
and a sense of direction. It involves on one hand a willing
submission to time and yet on the other a refusal to play the
victim's role with regard to time. Time's other name is
change, and one must understand that change is not only
predictable and expected, but is frequently one of God's
most powerful instruments as He collaborates with us.

We must use our time wisely, recognizing that good stewardship requires effort and a strong will. A part of that stewardship means that we are to be sensitive to the present
rather than living in some other time mode.

We have also wasted too much time by chasing happiness
as though it were an end. We frequently discover late in life
that happiness is a by-product of commitment and a genuine desire to follow God's will as one's primary goal in life.
Happiness is not something we seek.

Our understanding of time is also expanded when we hold

on to our dreams. We might have to relearn to dream, something that came so naturally when we were young. Somewhere along the way we discovered that forfeiting our dreams might insulate us from disappointment and heartache. When we give up our dreams, we unnecessarily become persons of poverty.

We also discover that there is more than one way to measure time. The world around us might use one standard, but the Bible would support some other alternatives. The real measure of time occurs when life as we know it now is understood as a time to prepare for what may be the most real world of all.

We must also learn to simplify our lives. Routine panic characterizes our way of life. We can blame no one but ourselves, because we are our worst enemy. We create lifestyles for ourselves that require more than we can deliver. Our needs are basically simple. The complication is usually made by us.

Celebration is a discipline that encourages us to stop and take note of significant moments. Learning to celebrate will almost magically tie chunks of our time together. We stop, look, and claim the blessings that come our way. And most of all, we acknowledge God as the source of all the good things that we celebrate.

Another vital component of the journey involves learning how to wait. God does not always work on our schedule. Needless to say, God does not restrict His activity to the time schedule found within the pages of our daily calendar. No daily planner has ever been the limit of God's activity in our world.

To make these kinds of adjustments requires a great deal of effort. "Making friends" with time does not happen accidently. Honest desire must be the fuel that fires the engine. This perception of time also occurs when one recognizes that it is a spiritual journey as well. "Making friends" with time is an intensely theological issue. If time is God's instrument and we envision time as an enemy, then what are we saying about God in the process?

A Wind-up Toy

One night recently, I was watching television after the rest of the family had gone to bed. I happened to be watching an old black and white movie that was about as uninteresting as a movie could possibly be. I do not remember the story line or who the characters were, but I do remember a scene that occurred early in the movie, and it made a rather strong image in my mind.

The scene was simple but quite symbolic. The camera was focused upon a young boy who had a wind-up toy soldier. In the scene the boy was continually winding up the toy soldier and watching it run down. His mother asked the boy what he was doing, and he replied, "I just enjoy watching him run down." That was the line, nothing more. But, within that frame I sensed more than just a boy's explanation of what he was doing.

I believe his words describe how most of us envision God's relationship to the world. Somewhere in our past we have been taught that God enjoys winding us up and watching us run down. Is life a just game? Is God the score keeper and the time keeper as well? Does He change the rules as we go, giving some creature more time than others, while He takes time from the unlucky ones? Have we come to perceive God as some kind of sadistic creature who finds pleasure in watching His creatures run out of time? Where did we ever develop such an erroneous understanding of God? It certainly was not from the Bible.

Yet, is that not where most of us spend our days and nights? We believe that God is somewhere just waiting for us to run down. He then smiles and points to us as He scratches off another one of His short-lived creatures. I am convinced that a new image is needed at this point, because this is not the God described in the Bible. And if we are ever to change time from the status of enemy to friend, we must go back to the source of much of our problem. That source is not God but the way we perceive Him and hesitate to trust Him.

The Centrality of Trust

In my book, *Hurry Up and Rest*, which dealt with the issue of learning how to rest, the last chapter dealt with the fact that, regardless of one's personal discipline, rest will never occur until one recognizes that there must be something beyond us to undergird life. If we believe that the fate of the world is totally upon our shoulders, rest will never occur. We must, somehow, learn to place our trust in a God who is still in control of the world, or there will never be any rest or peace. The key word is not *rest* or *peace*. The key word is *trust*. The same issue is before us in our efforts to become friends with time.

I have said on so many occasions and believe in the depths of my soul that trust is the foremost issue of our faith. Learning to love God and others is one of life's great challenges. The strength of our faith rests on our willingness to trust. Without a sense of trust, we will be at odds with time and the events that surround us. Trust is a part of our language. We spend our entire life talking and singing about it. Yet, most of us have never learned to trust the God who created us in His image.

Is our concept of God so small that we think He must diminish us in order to boost His own ego? How can we read the creation story in Genesis and share the Creator's exhilaration and then assume that He is playing a little game with us as He watches the personal clock for each of us run down like the toy soldier in the movie?

I am convinced that most of us find it difficult to trust

God. We might not confess it openly before our friends and family; but, for too many of us, the truth is obvious. If time is to ever become a friend, we must learn to trust the One who is "the beginning and the end."

There Is More

Learning to trust means that we believe that there is more to life than what we can see and touch. Our senses are so bound up with time. We watch our parents become older. Our own bodies change. The world is constantly changing. We seem imprisoned by time. History has been compared to a one way street. There is only one direction. We move through time at a prescribed pace. There is no slowing down or turning back. Is there anything beyond this forced march? The answer is a loud "yes!" But, only if we trust the One who is not imprisoned by history.

One of my seminary professors once called attention to the fact that Genesis claims, "In the beginning God." It does not read, "In the beginning time God." Time is real to God, but God is above and beyond it as the Creator. He cannot be bound by time which He created.

At the present moment we are within time, yet the Bible is clear that Christ has already transcended it. If we believe what we read and trust what God has said, then we also transcend time as well when we are in Christ. Does that mean that we will not face death or experience a final moment on this earth? Earthly death will still be a part of our experience. But, earthly death does not equal destruction.

God is above and beyond time. For Him there is no present tense that crumbles away as history moves along. For Him there is no past, present, or future. This does not mean that there is no existence. Existence is no longer framed by time. Through what God has done in Christ for us, we too become heirs to that same kind of existence, one that is unrelated to time.

John described God as the One "who created heaven, and the things that therein are, and the earth, and the things that therein are, and the sea, and the things which are therein, that there should be time no longer" (Rev. 10:6, KJV). "Time no longer." Such a thought might seem strange at first. Does that mean that all existence will cease? Absolutely not! Time will no longer exist, but life and existence will continue. Time is the frame that surrounds us in this stage of our life. There will come a day when we will toss away time like a butterfly tosses away a cocoon that housed life in the previous stage. Life will no longer be framed by time. Life is eternal, but time is temporary.

If we prefer to envision time as a straight line, then we must include on that line a beginning and an end. It is only the beginning and end of time, however, not God nor our existence with Him. The Bible teaches that Christ is "the beginning and the end." It was "in the fullness of the time" that God sent His Son (Gal. 4:4). Christ becomes the goal of history, and everything as we know it now is moving toward that moment. When that moment arrives, existence will not cease. Only time will be no more.

Time has a beginning and an end. Life in Christ is not bound by time. If we feel imprisoned by time, it is a temporary condition. What we see and touch is not all there is to life. It is only what we see and touch at the moment. The unseen world is unbound by time. I am totally convinced that the unseen world is the most real world of all. Someday we will discover that fact for ourselves.

More Than a Game

Most of us have never gotten beyond the suspicion that God is playing some kind of game with us. He tosses us onto the gameboard. He might have good intentions for us when

He starts to play with us, but sooner or later the toy becomes old and uninteresting. As interest wanes, He then either plays a sadistic game with us or, at best, removes us from the board and starts over with another new toy. In the meantime we are struggling every minute just to remain a part of the game. Our anxiety increases with every passing minute.

Once when I was a young boy I received for Christmas an electric football game. It was not the high-tech kind of electric games that are popular today. This game had two teams of plastic football players on a metal gameboard. The board vibrated and the players would move around, usually forward. I loved the game but usually became bored with it after a while, because it required so much effort to set the players up for each play. As a result I would frequently veer away from the regular game and play silly games with the players. I would arrange them to move around in little circles. I would tire of keeping up with all of them and use only a few of the faster ones. I would even break little pieces off of some of the players and watch them lay on their sides vibrating on the board with no predictable sense of direction. There were times when I would turn the power off and push the gameboard under my bed where it would remain forgotten for months and, in some cases, years.

Do We Really Trust?

Do we envision God as playing the same kind of games with us? Without a courageous sense of trust we will unquestionably perceive God as treating us like His toys. Our lives are not played on some giant gameboard where we vibrate around waiting on God to tire of us and either remove us from the board or shove the whole thing under some giant bed. The issue is once again, "Do we trust God?"

We can buy every time-management book on the market. We can try every form of meditation to slow down the pace of time. We can trade in our inexpensive watch for an expensive one. We can have a face-lift or an elbow tuck to deny our age. We can try every gimmick known to humankind to slow the effects of time upon our lives. But, unless we learn to trust God and believe that He is personally involved in the moving of events in our lives, we will still perceive time as an enemy rather than a friend. In so doing, we will not only be found guilty of fighting with time but with the "Lord of Time" as well.

In the nineteenth century Rev. Frederick D. Maurice wrote to his congregation and said:

> God has brought us into this time; He, not ourselves or some dark demon. If we are not fit to cope with that which He has prepared for us, we should have been utterly unfit for any condition that we imagine for ourselves. In this time we are to live and wrestle, and in no other. Let us humbly, tremblingly, manfully look at it, and we shall not wish that the sun could go back its ten degrees, or that we could go back with it. If easy times are departed, it is that the difficult times may make us more in earnest; that they may teach us not to depend upon ourselves. If easy belief is impossible, it is that we may learn what belief is, and in whom it is to be placed.[1]

The real issue at hand is that of trust, ultimate trust in the God of creation. Trust is not only one of the most significant issues of our faith but is undeniably bound with our efforts to make friends with time. Do you really trust God? Notice that I did not ask if you could sing the old hymns about trust or if you could speak the religious language. Do you really trust Him? Do you believe that God is a living, loving, and powerful Person who takes pleasure in every living creature? Do you believe that God takes pleasure in your joy and genuinely wants you to be a happy person? Or do you believe that God is playing some kind of game with you as He winds you up and watches you run down? Trust is the bottom line.

A Final Thought

In assessing my own thoughts and feelings after these pages, I discover that I am left with good news and bad news. The bad news is that time is still going to fly, whether I am having fun or not. The good news is that it doesn't matter. I'm on a journey that has purpose. There is meaning to it that is presently hidden from me.

For the moment I must trust the One who created the time which temporarily surrounds me and wait until the day when I will toss this way of living aside like an old shirt and move into a new way of existing that will make sense out of today's mysteries. In the meantime I will make the most and the best out of a fast moving world.

As I bring these pages to a conclusion, I find that my position actually surprises me. Instead of a lot of fancy advice that I thought I would be able to offer, I find a certain sense of peace about the passing of time. Time does fly when you're having fun and when you're not. So what?

Note

1. Mary Wilder Tileston, *Daily Strength for Daily Needs* (New York: Grosset and Dunlap, 1884), 37.